Icebreakers Galore!

The Ultimate
Game Guide for Girlfriends

Group

Loveland, Colorado

Icebreakers Galore!
The Ultimate Game Guide for Girlfriends
Copyright © 2008 Group Publishing, Inc.

Visit our Web site: **www.group.com/women**

Credits
Editor: Jill "I Spy" Wuellner
Project Manager: Amber "Scrabble" Van Schooneveld
Executive Developer: Amy "Hoopla" Nappa
Chief Creative Officer: Joani "Bingo!" Schultz
Copy Editor: Ann "Monopoly" Jahns
Cover Art Director/Designer and Art Director: Andrea "Rummy" Filer
Book Designer and Print Production Artist: Kadence "Scattergories" Ainsworth
Production Manager: DeAnne "Kick Ball" Lear

Icebreakers galore : the ultimate game guide for girlfriends / [editor, Jill Wuellner].
    p. cm.
Includes index.
ISBN-13: 978-0-7644-3625-3 (pbk. : alk. paper)
1. Church work with women. I. Wuellner, Jill.
BV4445.I24 2007
259.082--dc22

                      2007020833
ISBN 978-0-7644-3625-3

10 9 8 7 6 5 4 3 2 1   17 16 15 14 13 12 11 10 09 08
Printed in the United States of America.

Mixers

Icebreakers

Contents

Games With a Purpose

Just for Fun

Seasonal Games

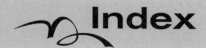# Index

Contents

Introduction

"When the working day is done, Girls—they want to have fun."

This line from the popular song by Cyndi Lauper, "Girls Just Want to Have Fun," does say a lot about women. Perhaps fun isn't *all* that we want, but it sure is part of the package!

While we love fun, it looks different for women than it does for children and teenagers. But if you've ever tried to find games for a group of women to play, you know it can be a difficult task. How many times have you found yourself flipping through an activity book for high-schoolers in an attempt to find a game for your group of girlfriends? While those games are certainly fun, they aren't typically what women want to play. We love chocolate, but not dripping from our hair. Some of us enjoy playing softball, but not necessarily with a wet sponge. And most of us get a good laugh from running in a relay race, but not when it includes eating whole onions or sitting on water balloons until they pop.

This is why we've created *Icebreakers Galore!* It's a book specifically for women, full of games and activities to play with girlfriends. Some are rowdy and packed with energy, while others are quiet and full of thoughtful questions. Whether you're planning a retreat, planning a shower, needing an icebreaker for a meeting, or just having some girlfriends over for a get-together, these games will help you plan the perfect event.

Inside you'll find games sorted into chapters, including:

• Mixers—for when you want to introduce everyone and start building friendships.

• Icebreakers—these are great for starting a meeting or an event.

• Games With a Purpose—activities to start a discussion or introduce a specific topic.

• Just for Fun Games—use these for retreats or events where you want everyone laughing and having side-splitting fun.

• Seasonal Games—to celebrate holiday events or get everyone prepared for a new season.

While some games and activities will require a bit of prep, *Icebreakers Galore!* includes many games that require little or no prep at all, which are great for those days when nothing is going right and you need a quick fix or you're asked to lead an activity at the last second. If you see this icon it means all you'll need are chairs and possibly some paper and pencils. No photocopying, shopping, gathering, or cutting required.

So go ahead and pick out a game to try with a group of girlfriends this week. Not only will you connect and deepen friendships, but you'll have a great time doing it.

NO PREP

Chapter 1
Mixers

The games and activities in this chapter are designed to help girlfriends get to know each other and make connections with other women. Whether it's simply learning names, hobbies, or things you have in common, these will get everyone talking and sharing part of who they are. These are perfect for groups that are just starting, if you have new women coming to an existing group, or when you want to just get to know each other a little bit better.

Middle Name Intros

How many girlfriends have wished, especially when they were younger, that they could choose their own name? Well, here's their opportunity.

NO PREP

Give girlfriends a minute or two to come up with an original middle name. This name should describe something about them. For example, "Audrey Hepburn" could describe someone who enjoys fine jewelry. "Martha Stewart" could identify a girlfriend who enjoys crafting, "Tiger Woods" could be a golf fanatic, or "Mozart" could identify someone who enjoys classical music.

Then go around the circle and have girlfriends introduce themselves, explaining their new middle names.

Personal Stories

Before your meeting, fill a bag with miscellaneous, ordinary items, such as a comb, a match, a leaf, a toothbrush, a fork, and so on.

Have your girlfriends sit in a circle, and ask the first one to reach into the bag and take the first thing she touches. Give her two minutes to tell a personal story that's related to that item. Then go around the circle, repeating this process, until everyone has selected an item and told a story that an item brought to mind.

If a woman has a hard time thinking of a story, suggest story themes that the items might inspire, such as a bad hair day (comb), a campfire mishap or burning a meal (match), a nature experience (leaf), a personal hygiene faux pas (toothbrush or deodorant), or a restaurant encounter (fork).

Encourage your group by going first!

Third Person

NO PREP

This is a simple activity you can use to make getting-to-know-you quite interesting!

Gather women in a circle for this Q-and-A crowd breaker—the catch is they have to answer questions in the third wwwhhwwof using "I"). Use fun questions such as these:

- Tell a story about a time when you met someone famous.

- Describe your ultimate date night.

- Talk about the earliest memory you have.

- Explain how you would prepare for a job interview with Steven Spielberg or Bill Gates.

- Talk about the strangest thing that's ever happened to you.

Not only will everyone get a chuckle from hearing people talk about themselves this way, but the group will also get to hear each person's name numerous times.

Top~Secret Missions

Create a bonding experience for women with this getting-to-know-you mixer.

Supplies

• *3x5 cards*

Before your meeting, you'll need to come up with one "secret mission" for each member of your group and write it on a 3x5 card. Each secret mission should somehow encourage women to interact with others. Use the following suggestions or create your own:

• Meet someone new, and find out where her shoes came from.

• Compliment five people (be specific and genuine).

• Find a girlfriend who hasn't finished her secret mission, and help her finish it.

• Give five people a high five.

• Introduce two women who don't know each other very well.

• Find something you have in common with three other people (all four of you have the same thing in common).

• Get someone to sing to you—any song will do!

• Meet a new girlfriend, and learn the names of her siblings.

As girlfriends arrive, hand each one a secret mission. Tell them they must secretly accomplish their missions without revealing to the others what their missions actually are. You'll want to give group members about 10 minutes to complete their tasks. Afterward, discuss what they learned about each other and whether they succeeded in accomplishing their missions.

Scripture Mixer

Prior to your meeting, you will need to write out portions of well-known Scripture on slips of paper.

As women arrive, hand out the slips of paper, and let everyone roam about introducing themselves to each other, telling their piece of Scripture. If a woman finds someone she belongs with, they should stick together until they complete the Scripture. For instance, someone with a slip reading, "Even though I walk through the valley of the shadow of death" must find the person with, "I fear no evil, for you are with me," and the other people with the rest of Psalm 23 (NIV).

Supplies

- *slips of paper with Scripture written on them*

Game Tip:

Because this game requires players to have some Bible knowledge, it's a good one to use before a Bible study. You might even use the passages that have been studied in previous weeks!

Junk Mixer

This is a good mixer if you are starting a new group or have new girlfriends coming to an existing group.

For this activity, you will need to collect small household items, such as a button, eraser, rubber band, thimble, emery board, pencil, or Popsicle stick. You'll need one item for each girlfriend. List the items on a sheet of paper with a line beside each item, and make a photocopy for each person.

Place each item in an envelope, and as women arrive, hand them each an envelope and a photocopied list. Explain that each girlfriend must somehow wear her item. Women will then mingle, find out who's wearing each item, and write that person's name in the appropriate place on the list.

Supplies

- *envelopes, items as described in the game*
- *photocopies of the list of items*
- *pens and pencils*

Game Tip:

This game can easily be adapted for a baby shower by using items such as a pacifier, a diaper, a baby washcloth, a baby sock, a tiny nail clipper, and other small baby items.

If You...

Supplies

- *chairs*

NO PREP

Have girlfriends sit in a circle. You'll have one fewer chair than you have players, and the player without a chair must stand in the middle of the circle. Explain that you're going to read a series of statements that all begin with "If you…" When you say "Go," everyone who has done what the statement describes must find a new place to sit, leaving a new person in the middle.

This is one of those games that really doesn't have a winner, so you can play for as long as you have statements or questions. To add to the fun, try to include a few statements that you're sure include everyone, so the entire circle must get up and move. Here are a few to get you started:

- If you have ever fallen asleep in church…
- If you have ever burned your dinner…
- If you have ever spilled something in a restaurant…
- If you have ever slipped and fallen in a public place…
- If you have ever put your shoes on the wrong feet…
- If you like pineapple on your pizza…
- If you know Psalm 23 by heart…
- If you have ever had a "bad hair day"…
- If you can remember your first grade teacher's name…
- If you talk to plants…

Hot~Banana Talks

Most likely it's been a long time since you played a good game of Hot Potato. Well, put on your quick hands and sharpen your mind, because this is a similar game but with a twist that women will love.

When women arrive, give them each several 3x5 cards, and ask them to come up with a question for each card. Suggest questions that are both serious, such as "What's the most important thing in your life?" and questions that are silly, such as "What's your favorite kind of fast food?" When everyone is done with their questions, have them place the cards in a paper bag.

Have everyone sit in a circle, and begin tossing the banana while music plays from a CD. At random intervals, turn off the music and call out "Stop." Each time you call "Stop," the person holding the banana must answer a question from the bag. Repeat the process until everyone has had a chance to answer a question.

Supplies

- *banana*
- *3x5 cards*
- *pens or pencils*
- *paper bag*
- *CD player or radio*

Game Tip:

It's a good idea to use a firm, almost green banana for this game—or it might get messy!

Color Me Friend

You can use this colorful game to help women remember each other's names and learn something new about each other.

Hand each girlfriend a crayon, and explain that they're to look at the name of their crayon's color (some colors have pretty interesting names!). Next, have them arrange themselves in alphabetical order according to the name of the crayon color. When the line is complete, have girlfriends turn to the person on either side and tell something about themselves that reminds them of their color. For example, a woman might say, "Red—I love red roses," or "Blue—my favorite fruit is blueberries."

Supplies

- *crayons*

Game Tip:

Have girlfriends trade crayons and repeat the activity several times. Then collect the crayons. As you show the crayons one by one, have girlfriends share something they remember about another person that was related to that color.

When I Was a Kid

If you have dramatic girlfriends in your group, they'll love this game!

NO PREP

Have girlfriends form two teams of equal number. Tell teams that each person should come up with a memorable story from her childhood. The events can be funny, embarrassing, serious, or outlandish.

Give teams several minutes to meet and tell their stories. If possible, teams should meet away from each other, so they can't overhear each other's stories. Each team should then choose which stories they are going to share with the whole group. Teams should also decide who is going to relate which stories. The person telling the story can be the person who actually experienced it, or it can be someone who tries to convince the other team the incident actually happened to her.

When everyone is ready, call teams together, and have them take turns telling stories. After someone tells a story, the other team should try to guess who really experienced the incident. Teams get one point for every correct guess and one point for every time the other team guesses wrong. The team with the most points at the end wins.

Encourage women to really ham it up when they tell the stories. You can even have those drama queens act portions out or add sound effects!

Meet in the Middle

Women will discover how much they have in common during this simple game.

NO PREP

Have girlfriends form a circle. Explain that when you call out a phrase that describes them, they will walk to the middle of the circle and introduce themselves to everyone else in the middle. Start by naming items of clothing, such as bluejeans or a flowered shirt, and then move to hobbies or favorite foods they might have. You can also use phrases such as "one sibling," "loves cooking," or "book lover."

My Favorite Things

NO PREP

Here's a great game to help women make connections with other women who have the same interests and passions.

Have everyone stand in the middle of the room. Explain that you are going to read a list of categories. Each time you name a category, women must call out their favorite thing in that category. They will keep calling it out until they find other people who have the same favorite. For example, if you call out "movie," women will begin calling out the title of their favorite movie. Everyone who is calling out the name of the same movie can form a group. Inevitably there will be women who will be the only one with a favorite thing. That's OK. It's a good reminder of how diverse your group is and the unique interests of all girlfriends.

Here are some suggestions for categories you may wish to call out:

- lipstick (brand or color)
- dessert
- singer or band
- season
- color
- movie
- sport
- holiday

Lifelines

This is an activity that will take most of your meeting time, but it's well worth it as women bond and truly become girlfriends.

Supplies

- *butcher paper*
- *tape*
- *markers*
- *glue*
- *scissors*
- *magazines*
- *paper scraps*

You'll need to choose three or more rooms in your church or building, depending on the size of your group. Tape a continuous roll of butcher paper around the walls of each room. Mark the beginning of each decade at regular intervals along timelines, taking into consideration the ages of the women in your group (so if no one is older than 30 you won't need to go back to the 1920s to begin marking decades—but if you have women who were born in the 1920s, you'll want to be sure to start your decade markers then).

Divide women into smaller groups (it's best if groups are not bigger than four), and assign each group to one room that has been supplied with markers, paper scraps, glue, scissors, and magazines.

Have group members each make a timeline of their life by drawing or gluing scraps or magazine pictures on the paper. Tell them to start with their birth and draw events, people, and places that were important while they grew up. They'll all be using the same timeline—just putting their own key events along it. When they're done, have girlfriends tell their names and creatively share their lifelines with the whole group (this means everyone will tour the timelines around the building).

I Remember...

Take a stroll down memory lane with this mixer.

Have girlfriends form a circle, and have them think back to when they were in kindergarten or younger, to the first thing they remember. Before women share their memories, let them take two minutes to search the room for a symbol that represents that memory. For example, a woman could choose a book to represent an early memory of a grandparent reading a bedtime story.

NO PREP

After two minutes, gather back in a circle and share your names, memories, and symbols. It's fun to hear what everyone remembers from young ages!

Bowl Me Over!

This game is great for groups of up to 10. If you have a larger group of women, make several bowling sets and place them around your room.

Supplies

- *10 empty toilet paper tubes*
- *a 12-inch or larger rubber ball*
- *strips of paper*
- *tape*
- *pen or pencil*

Before your meeting, you'll need to write one of the following phrases on the side of each tube: favorite musician, worst food, last vacation, dream car, a hobby, most dreaded chore, best vacation, worst date ever, favorite late-night snack, and favorite movie. Inside each tube, tape a slip of paper with one of the following items written on it: age, birth city, nickname in junior high, silliest thing you ever did, favorite TV show as a teenager, something your parents said that you hated to hear, best advice you ever received, your best attribute, age when you became a Christian, and your most interesting job.

Set up the tubes like bowling pins about 9 inches apart. Give one girlfriend the ball, and have her stand 10 to 15 feet from the "pins." Then have her try to bowl down as many pins as possible. The bowler will share responses to the statements on the outside of the tubes left standing. If all the tubes are knocked down, the bowler will pick a tube and ask another girl-friend to share her response to the question inside that tube.

• • •

The Shoe Pile

NO PREP

It's a well-known fact that women love shoes, so why not use them to help women get to know each other better?

Have participants walk around the room, talking to each other and finding out as much about others as they can. Suggest that they ask about each others' favorites—vacation spots, authors, or movies, for example. After about five minutes, call everyone together, and ask each woman to put one shoe into a pile. Then have everyone sit in a circle and try to hide her other shoe by sitting on that foot or tucking the foot behind a purse or covering it with a sweater (so others can't use it as a clue to figure out whom the missing shoe belongs to). Have one person at a time go to the shoe pile, select a shoe that belongs to someone else, try to match it to its owner, and then tell what she learned about that person. You can also ask other women to contribute facts they learned about that person as well.

A Spy for a Spy

James Bond, watch out. Help new girlfriends meet the "regulars" with this sneaky mixer.

Before you begin, secretly choose three women to be spies. Give them code names, such as "Pink Panther," "007," or "Maxwell Smart."

Instruct participants that their mission is to find the three spies. They'll have several minutes to mingle. Women must each approach a person, shake hands, and ask her name. Then, while still holding hands, they must ask if she is either the Pink Panther, 007, or Maxwell Smart. So as not to be too obvious, they may ask only one code name at a time. A "no" response is one squeeze of the hand; a "yes" response is two squeezes of the hand.

When women catch a spy, they shouldn't reveal the spy's identity but continue meeting others. When a person thinks she has discovered the true identity of all three spies, she must report to "headquarters" (the leader) and reveal the spies' names. The first person to learn all three spies' real names wins.

Reward the champion spy-catcher with an appropriate prize, such as a squirt gun, sunglasses, or a magnifying glass.

Stand~Up Show and Tell

Girlfriends will certainly enjoy this activity that brings back such fond memories of childhood.

Have girlfriends choose something they are wearing or something they have brought with them. Explain that you'd like them to think about why the items they chose are special to them or part of their identities. For example, someone might share about a necklace that belonged to her grandmother, and another might talk about a special picture in her wallet.

Then ask girlfriends to Show and Tell one at a time.

Encourage other participants to ask questions, and give everyone a chance to present her special item.

Cut From a Different Dough

This mixer is not only a creative way for girlfriends to get to know each other—it's also yummy and smells delicious!

To begin, spread store-bought cookie dough onto a 13x9 baking sheet, and bake according to package directions. As the cookie dough is baking, have girlfriends peruse the assortment of cutters, frostings, and decorations that are available for them to use, and have each one select a cutter that characterizes her in some way. If you are using this game during the holidays, have them choose a cutter that depicts a favorite part of the holiday season.

Shortly after removing the cookies from the oven, have your girlfriends each cut out a cookie from the baked dough and take a few minutes to decorate it. When everyone is done, ask them to explain why they chose the cutter they did.

Supplies

- *sugar-cookie dough*
- *cookie cutters of different shapes*
- *cookie sheets, and an assortment of frostings*
- *sprinkles, and other decorative edibles*

Game Tip:

This activity can be used any time of year or adapted for the holidays by using cookie cutters specific to a holiday or season.

Pet Talk

Will the real pet owner please stand up? If you'd like your girlfriends to learn more about each other, then let their pets do the talking!

Have girlfriends each write on a 3x5 card the names of their pets. If someone doesn't have a pet, she can write the name of a pet she had as a child, or the name of a pet she wishes she had.

Then form teams of four or more, and have each team mix up their cards among themselves. Call the teams, one by one, to stand in front of the others and read their team's cards with the names of the pets. The other teams must guess which pet names belong to which team members. Repeat the process until all teams have finished.

Award fun pet prizes, such as dog biscuits or pet toys, for the best name, for the funniest name, and to the woman whose pet name was easiest to match to her.

Your group is sure to discover hilarious pet names and learn new secrets about one another.

Supplies

- *3x5 cards*
- *pens or pencils*

What's My Name?

This is a game that has many variations. It can be played using characters from pop culture (such as Mickey Mouse, Michael Jackson, and Jennifer Aniston), history (Abraham Lincoln, Betsy Ross, and Benjamin Franklin), or the Bible (David, Deborah, and Abraham). Any way it's played is great fun.

Beforehand, you will need to write the names of characters you will be using on pieces of paper. Make one name for each woman participating.

As women arrive, have them fill out a name tag to attach to the front of their shirts. Tape one prepared name to each woman's back, but don't let her see the name (so the front of her shirt will show her real name, and her back will show the character name).

The object of the game is to ask questions to find out who the character is on your back. Participants can only ask "yes" or "no" questions. While they can ask as many questions as they like, they can only ask one question at a time. After a woman asks someone a question, she must find someone else to question before returning to the previous person.

Additionally, participants must use the real name of the person they are speaking to every time they ask a question. For example, a woman could ask, "Tammy, am I a movie star?" This means if she forgets to use the real first name, the other woman should not answer the question.

Once a woman thinks she knows the name on her back, she can ask someone and get a "yes" or "no" answer.

Supplies

- *paper*
- *tape*
- *name tags*
- *pens or pencils*

Game Tip:

It's helpful if women know the category of names they are choosing from. So if you stick with cartoon characters, famous actresses, or people from the Bible, let women know the overall category so they'll at least have an idea that they're looking for Wilma Flintstone instead of George Washington.

Roll a Conversation

Game Tip:

If you're short on time, don't create the conversation cubes. Instead, write a numbered list of the questions for each team, and then give them a die instead of a box. Teams will discuss the questions on their lists that correspond with the numbers on the die.

To prepare for this game, you will need to make "Conversation Cubes" by closing the small boxes and wrapping each one with newsprint. You will then need to write one of the following questions on each side of the box:

- What's your favorite holiday? Why?
- If you had a million dollars to spend, what would you buy?
- If you could have dinner with anyone, alive or dead, who would it be? Why?
- What's the Bible story that means the most to you? Explain.
- Tell about a special family memory.
- What is your greatest strength?

Have participants form groups of four, and give each group a box. Explain that they are going to get to know each other a bit better by using the "Conversation Cubes." The group will need to introduce themselves and have a girlfriend "roll" the cube. The question that's on the top when the cube stops rolling is the question everyone in the group will take turns answering. Groups will only have two minutes, so encourage women to try and give as many people the opportunity to answer as possible.

After two minutes, have girlfriends mingle and then form new groups of four. Have them repeat the process, giving them two minutes to introduce themselves and answer a question.

Gab Bag

This game is certain to get women laughing as they share their own stories with each other.

Supplies

• one "Gab Bag" game per six women. *Order these purse-sized games at www.group.com/ women.*

Have women sit in circles of five or six. Give each group one Gab Bag game. The first person rolls both cubes and reads the two words that are showing. Then that woman shares a story, a memory, or whatever thought comes to her mind based on those two words. For example, if the words that are showing are *sweet* and *food,* she might share about her favorite sweet food, a food that makes her feel sweet, a sweet gift of food someone once gave her, or a food that she thinks is too sweet to eat. It's that easy!

Game Tip:

You can play this game anywhere! Store one in your purse to play over coffee with girlfriends at a local shop, tuck one in the glove compartment of your car to play on road trips, or use one with your family around the table to get new conversations started.

Then the cubes are passed to the next person who rolls them and shares based on the words she rolled. Continue as long as time permits, making sure each woman has at least two turns. If women roll the same combination of words twice, they can come up with new ways to use those combinations. For example, *best* and *friend* will obviously lead women to share about their own best friends. But they could also tell about a best friend from grade school, the best quality a friend could have, the best time shared with a friend, and so on. Challenge women to think again for a new way to use the combinations if they roll the same one twice.

Ping~Pong Popcorn

Supplies

- *masking tape*
- *pencils*
- *one plastic spoon*
- *one Ping-Pong ball per girlfriend*

To prepare for this game, you will need to divide your playing area in half by placing a masking tape strip across the middle of the floor. Distribute pencils and Ping-Pong balls, and have each girlfriend write her name on a ball. Then have girlfriends form two groups, and have groups move to opposite sides of the playing area and sit so they're facing the other group.

Next, you'll give each girlfriend a plastic spoon. Explain that when you give the signal, they can use their spoons to launch the Ping-Pong balls across the room. They should continue launching other Ping-Pong balls that come their way back to the other side of the room. Explain that when you call time, girlfriends should grab the closest ball and hold on to it.

Let them launch the Ping-Pong balls and continue play for about 30 seconds. Call time and wait for everyone to grab a ball. Then instruct girlfriends to quickly find the person whose name is on the ball they're holding and tell that person their favorite food from childhood.

Have girlfriends play again, but change the information they must exchange. You might have them tell their favorite flavor of ice cream, favorite vacation spot, the last movie they saw, or about the first car they owned.

Common Bonds

NO PREP

This is an interesting way for girlfriends to get to know each other a little better.

Before starting this game, explain that you are going to call out categories and then divisions within each category. Each girlfriend will need to go to the category division that best fits her. Once everyone is in her division, you will read a question, and everyone will take turns answering it within her group.

Begin by calling out the first category, and then tell girlfriends where each division within that category should go. After girlfriends form their divisions, ask your question. When everyone has had a chance to answer the question, move on to the second category and its divisions.

Following are some examples of categories, divisions, and questions. Feel free to add to the list.

Category 1—Birth order

- Divisions: oldest, middle child, youngest, only child
- Question: Describe the member of your family you are most like.

Category 2—Length of residence in the area

- Divisions: my whole life, about half my life, less than a quarter of my life, I'm new here
- Question: What do you remember about the day you moved here?

Category 3—Free time

- Divisions: read a book, spend time with friends, go shopping, watch TV
- Question: What's your favorite hobby or interest?

Category 4—Vacation destination

- Divisions: home, the sunny beach, the mountains, a chocolate factory
- Question: What's your favorite vacation location?

Pass the Beans

Everyone has a special talent and unique experiences, but sometimes they are hidden, so no one else knows about them. The goal of this game is to reveal those gifts to the rest of the group.

Ask women to form groups of five, and then have each group sit in a circle. Give each person 15 beans. Explain that girlfriends are to try and collect beans by describing their unique experiences or abilities. For example, a woman might tell about running in a marathon, being able to recite all the books of the Bible, or her passion for painting with watercolors. Whatever activity they describe must be absolutely true.

After someone shares a unique activity or ability, each girlfriend who hasn't done that activity or doesn't have that ability must give that person one bean. Have participants take turns listing their unique experiences and abilities until each person has shared 10 activities.

After everyone in each group has listed 10 activities, ask women to report how many beans they've collected. Then ask for volunteers to share interesting activities they heard about, and encourage women who have done an activity that was reported about to tell about their experiences.

Supplies

- *15 dried beans for each person participating*

Game Tip:

If you don't have beans handy, you can use pennies, marbles, toothpicks, or any other small and easy-to-find object.

Sign Up

This is a quick and easy game that will get girlfriends moving around and interacting with everyone.

Before your meeting, photocopy the "Sign Up" handout. Give each woman a copy, and tell girlfriends they must find someone for each item on the list. Participants can ask a person only one question at a time. If the answer is "no," she must go to someone else before returning with another question. If the answer is "yes," have the person sign on the line next to the item. After 10 minutes, the woman with the most signatures is the winner.

Supplies

- *photocopy of handout*
- *pens or pencils*

Game Tip:

This game can be easily adapted for larger or smaller groups by creating a list that states characteristics that are specific to the women in your group.

Sign Up

_____ I use red toothpaste.

_____ I watch *Sesame Street.*

_____ I read the comics in the newspaper every day.

_____ I was born over 1,000 miles from here.

_____ I listen to classical music regularly.

_____ I like to play chess.

_____ I squeeze the toothpaste in the middle.

_____ I like to eat sushi.

_____ I have traveled overseas.

_____ I like to watch suspenseful movies.

_____ I have no cavities in my teeth.

_____ I don't like coffee.

_____ I consider chocolate a food group.

_____ I dance the "Macarena."

_____ I lie about my age.

I've Got Your Number

Supplies

- *sticky name tags*
- *marker*
- *slips of paper*

Game Tip:

For extra fun, call out more than one number at a time. You may even want to prepare more than one instruction for each number and let the game continue!

Before the meeting, you'll need to prepare a name tag for each girlfriend, but instead of writing her name, write a number. Then, prepare a slip of paper for each person with instructions written on it, making sure you have an instruction for each number. The instructions might include the following: "Introduce 4 to 3," "Shake hands with 3 and 6," "Find out what 2 likes best for breakfast," and "Discover 7's birthday."

Give each woman a name tag with a number on it when she arrives, and ask her to place the name tag where everyone can see it. Then have women stand in a circle, and give each person a slip of paper with an instruction written on it.

Explain that when you call out a number, the person with that number has to immediately carry out the instruction written on her slip of paper. As soon as she finishes and returns to her place in the circle, call out another number. Keep the game going at a fast pace until you've called out all the numbers in the circle.

Who? What? Where?

Supplies

- *photocopy of the "Who? What? Where?" handout, which has been cut apart into assignments*

Communication…many people would say women are excellent communicators, but all of us have trouble communicating with someone. Here's a great game to emphasize the necessity of good verbal and nonverbal communication.

Have girlfriends form five teams, and give each team one assignment from the "Who? What? Where?" handout. Tell team members that their job will be to involve the whole team in a 60-second pantomime of their assignment. They should do this in such a way that the rest of the group will be able to guess **who** they are pantomiming, **what** the person is doing, and **where** she is doing it.

Allow teams to find private places where they can practice their pantomimes. After five minutes, call the groups back together, and have teams perform their pantomimes one at a time. Encourage the other girlfriend groups to guess what each team is pantomiming.

Who? What? Where?

ASSIGNMENT 1

Who? A yodeler

What? Fending off a mouse that is creeping up her leg

Where? On a New York subway

ASSIGNMENT 2

Who? A clown

What? Crossing a river filled with alligators

Where? A zoo

ASSIGNMENT 3

Who? An elephant

What? Eating cotton candy

Where? At a gas station

ASSIGNMENT 4

Who? A church choir member

What? Carrying a water balloon

Where? On a bed of hot coals

ASSIGNMENT 5

Who? A small girl

What? Balancing a soft-drink bottle in her hand

Where? On a train track

More Than You Know

This activity makes mingling mandatory and also gives women a chance to toot their own horns!

Supplies

- card stock paper
- scissors
- a hole punch
- yarn
- markers
- pens

Game Tip:

If you have more than 30 women, you might want to form two groups for this so it doesn't take as long for the sharing time.

Using the supplies listed, as women arrive, have each one make a big name tag to hang around her neck. They should then sit in a circle so all the name tags are visible.

Give each person a pen and another piece of stiff paper. Instruct everyone to list all the other women's names on their paper. After listing everyone's name, women are to walk around and find out one thing about each person and write it beside her name. Explain that each time they are asked for information, their answer must be different. They can't tell any two people the same thing! The challenge is for women to try to complete their lists while not repeating themselves.

When everyone's finished, return to the circle to share your discoveries. Begin with the first name on your list, and tell what you found out about her. Then have the person to your right say what she found out about that person, and continue around the circle until it gets back to you.

Then go to the next name on your list, and again go around the circle. Do this until everyone's name and information has been read. This activity is well worth the extra time it takes. Women will discover a lot of "in commons" with each other for future conversations.

Trivia Scavenger Hunt

This is a game for all your trivia buffs, and it is a fun way to integrate and introduce multigenerational groups.

Supplies

- *pens or pencils*
- *3x5 cards*

Before the game, write trivia questions on index cards. You'll need three questions on each card and one card for each participant, using each question only once. For example, you might ask questions such as, "What are the names of three characters on *Sesame Street*?" or "Who was the U.S. president who preceded Lyndon Johnson?" You can find good trivia questions by using a Trivial Pursuit game or books on trivia and topics like pop culture, sports, or history.

To begin the game, give each woman a card and a pen or pencil. Have everyone write her name on her card. Explain that, as in a scavenger hunt, players must locate items. However, in this game, "items" are the people who possess the answers to the trivia questions on the cards. Players will need to assess the questions to determine who in the room is most likely to know the answer to each question.

In the game, everyone is free to move about the room asking questions, but a player may ask only one question of a person at a time. If a woman wants to ask more than one question of another girlfriend, she must first ask a question of someone else and then return to ask a second question of the first person.

Additionally, a girlfriend can only give another person one answer, so three different people answer the questions on the card. When a woman finds someone to give her an answer, she must write down that person's name.

When players have acquired answers to their questions, have them sit down. Even after they've completed their cards, others still seeking answers can approach them.

When all the cards are completed, each girlfriend should tell the answers to her trivia questions and introduce the people who provided her with the knowledge she sought.

Hoop It Up

Supplies

- *one Hula-Hoop for every two or three women*

Most of us played with Hula-Hoops as children, and while it would be hilarious to see girlfriends try to use them as adults, here's a more practical use for this childhood favorite.

Place the Hula-Hoops on the floor around your meeting area. Gather girlfriends in a circle in the center of the room, and explain that when you say, "Hoop it up," they must go to any one of the Hula-Hoops and stand in its center, with no more than three women in a hoop. Tell them to bring the hoop up around themselves, if possible, to make them into a tight little group. Then read a statement, and have women take three minutes (one minute per person) to share information with their group. When you say, "Hoop it up" again, girlfriends will put the hoop down and form new groups with different people in a different hoop.

Read one of these statements each time women form a new hooped group:

- Tell an early memory you have about going to a doctor or dentist.
- Tell what your toughest school subject was and why.
- Tell one dream you have for your life.
- Tell about your favorite Bible person (other than Jesus) and why he or she is your favorite.

Chapter 2
Icebreakers

Icebreakers are great for groups of all sizes and seasons. They can be used to begin a meeting with a bit of fun, to get everyone mingling, or to get girlfriends moving and laughing when the sugar coma sets in after snack time.

Human Tick~Tack~Toe

The ancient game of Tick-Tack-Toe can take on new excitement in your group of girlfriends by making it life-size.

You'll need to set up nine chairs in three rows, just like the sections on a Tick-Tack-Toe diagram. Then divide your group into two teams. Each team takes its turn by sending one person to sit in a selected chair. The first team to get three in a row wins. Beware, since you're not using X's and O's, this can get confusing and laughter will ensue!

To make it a bit more exciting, establish a time limit during which each team member has to select a seat. Give each woman, say, five seconds after the last girlfriend sat down to reach the chosen chair.

Supplies

- *nine chairs*

NO PREP

In My Day

Supplies

- *index cards*
- *pens or pencils*

This is a fun and interesting game if your group is made up of women from varying age groups.

Begin by asking participants to divide into two teams: Everyone over 40 on one team, and everyone under 40 on the other team. Each team should be supplied with index cards and pens or pencils.

Each team will need to write down clues pertaining to various items or terms commonly used in their generation. For example, the over-40 group might write, "This word was commonly used in the 1960s and 1970s; this word also sounds similar to what one would find on a vinyl record. Answer: groovy." The under-40 group might write, "This item was a doll we played with and is also a scrumptious dessert. Answer: Strawberry Shortcake."

When teams have finished writing clues, give them an opportunity to quiz each other. If you like, keep score and see which generation is the most knowledgeable about the other. You might be surprised!

If teams need help coming up with clues, you can give them these ideas: musical terms, slang terms, dress styles, cars, school subjects, dating terminology, and popular movies and books.

Eye Spy?

Supplies

- *a sheet with a small hole in the middle*

Game Tip:

If necessary, a large piece of cardboard in a doorway can be used to substitute for the sheet.

How well do you know your girlfriends? Could you pick them out by seeing just one feature?

For this activity you will need a sheet with a small hole near the middle of it. Hang the sheet from the ceiling, and have the group try to identify different girlfriends when only one feature, such as the eyes, mouth, or one hand is visible. Make sure the group cannot see the girlfriends as they line up behind the sheet.

Get~to~Know~You Toss

Supplies

• *three balls of different colors*

Have your group gather in a circle, and give three people each a ball. Ask them to throw the balls to others in the circle. The girlfriends who catch the balls must answer a question according to the color of the ball they've caught. So if you have a yellow, green, and red ball, the woman who catches the yellow ball might have to answer the question, "How many people are in your family, and what are their names?" The person who catches the green ball might have to answer, "What is your favorite coffee drink?" The person who catches the red ball might have to answer, "What's a funny memory or embarrassing moment you've had?"

Other suggestions for questions are:

• What's an unusual talent you have?

• What's the best vacation you've ever taken?

• What's your favorite holiday and why?

After the first three people have answered the questions, they throw the balls to three other women, who'll answer the questions according to the balls they catch. Continue until everyone has answered at least one question.

Trading Up

Game Tips:

If you have more than 13 women in your group, you'll need to add in a second deck of cards. If you have more than 23 women, you'll need three decks of cards, and so on.

To make the game a little more challenging, play the game with more decks, and have women match eight of a kind for double the fun!

This activity uses simple decks of playing cards and is a fun way to get girlfriends interacting.

Shuffle the cards and deal four cards to each woman. Tell players to look only at their own cards. Explain that when the game starts, players each have to trade their cards quickly with someone else who wants to trade the same number of cards. They'll know what cards they're trading, but they won't know what cards they're receiving until they've traded them. The object is for a player to continue "blind" trades until she has four matching cards.

When a player has four of a kind, she runs up to the leader and turns the cards in for a small reward. (Chocolate always works well with girlfriends!) Play until everyone has matched cards and received a reward.

Desperately Seeking Susan

Supplies

- photos of your girlfriends group
- scissors
- poster board
- glue
- crayons or markers
- list of people for girlfriends to find

Wondering what to do with all those photos you've taken from previous girlfriend gatherings and retreats? Well, grab a bunch of photos you've taken over a period of time, and cut around each woman in the pictures. On a poster board, create a background scene such as a beach, a mountain retreat, or a church auditorium. Glue the pictures of the women to this background scene, overlapping them to create a huge collage.

Then before your meeting, post a list of things to find. Your list may include items such as "Find Karen tying her shoe," "Find Pam," or "Find three women wearing red."

Your girlfriends will enjoy this pre-meeting activity and will have a few laughs at the new scenes created by this collage.

Up and Down Relay

Supplies
- *chairs*
- *paper*
- *pens or pencils*

It's always good to begin a Bible study with a review of what was covered in previous lessons, but review can be boring. So here's a way to review and have fun while doing it!

Have girlfriends form a single-file line facing a row of five chairs. Place a piece of paper and a pen or pencil on each chair. When you say "Go," the first person in line runs to the first chair, picks up the pencil and paper, sits down, and writes one word about the concept you were previously studying. For example, if in your previous meeting you were discussing walking by faith, women might write "trust," "lamp," "dark," "follow," or "choice."

When the first woman has written a word, she then gets out of the chair, placing the paper and pencil back on the seat, and repeats the same routine on each and every chair.

As soon as the first player in line sits in the second chair, the second player may go. The third person in line must watch for the second person to move to the second chair before she may go. The challenge is that women may not repeat a word that has already been written. The game continues until everyone has written a word on each list.

When everyone has had a turn, read the papers so everyone has a chance to be reminded of the lesson(s) previously learned.

Working Together

NO PREP

Use this game as a time-filler or as a way to get girlfriends interacting with each other. Have participants get into pairs, and then explain that they must create a "secret handshake." It can contain as many different moves and actions as they like; for example, high fives, knocking elbows, twirling in a circle, and snapping their fingers. Encourage them to try to be as creative as possible.

After each pair has had some time to create, have girlfriends demonstrate their handshakes. It's also fun to have them vote for the most creative, craziest, and longest handshakes.

Wacky Questions

NO PREP

This icebreaker is a great way to open a meeting, introduce girlfriends, and get everyone smiling. It also can be used over and over with simply a different question.

You'll want to have everyone stand or sit in a circle, state her name, and give a response to a wacky question, which may or may not be related to your meeting topic.

The possibilities for questions are endless, but here's a sample of some questions you might ask:

- What's your favorite product with milk in it?
- What's your favorite underarm deodorant, and which pit do you hit first?
- What's your favorite chore around the house?
- What's the grossest food you've ever eaten?
- What's the worst movie you've ever seen?
- Which side of the bed do you sleep on?
- What's the goofiest hairstyle you ever wore?

Jelly Bean Jam

Supplies
- *jelly beans*
- *envelopes*

To prepare for this activity, you will need to place nine jelly beans of different colors in an envelope for each girlfriend participating.

Just before the game, give an envelope of jelly beans to each girlfriend. The object of the game is to get nine jelly beans of the same color. Girlfriends have to ask others for the color jelly bean they want and then trade one of theirs. They may only trade one jelly bean at a time.

This activity takes time, because several girlfriends may be pursuing jelly beans of the same color. The first person to get to nine same-color jelly beans is the winner.

You can adapt this game with any candy that comes in many colors.

Quick Sort

NO PREP

This is a simple activity that will get women talking and moving around as well.

Have girlfriends form two teams. Explain that you are going to call out categories, and each team will need to sort itself as quickly as possible into a line in the order you have suggested. For example, if you say, "Sort by age, youngest to oldest," teams should form a line with the youngest person on one end and the oldest person on the other end.

Before keeping score, it would be a good idea to have several practice rounds and then award a point each round to the team that gets in line most quickly. Some categories might call for rough estimates, but teams should be able to defend their positions and orders.

Here are some sorting suggestions to get you started:

- Sort by height from shortest to tallest.
- Sort by shoe size from largest to smallest.
- Sort by the number of states you have visited, most states to fewest.
- Sort by the farthest distance ever traveled, farthest distance to shortest distance.
- Sort by the number of instruments you play, most to least.
- Sort by the number of times you've moved, least to most.
- Sort by the number of siblings you have, least to most.
- Sort by the number of sodas you drink in a day, most to least.
- Sort by the number of trees in your yard, most to least.
- Sort by the number of movies you've been to this year, least to most.
- Sort by the number of traffic violations you've had, most to least.

Icebreakers

Laws and Guffaws

Unwritten laws govern our everyday lives (it's rude to cut someone off in traffic; if someone doesn't answer the door, it's not polite to keep ringing the bell). Here's a game where women must discover what unwritten law is governing the game.

Choose two or three women to stand outside hearing distance of the rest of the group. The group must then decide on a "law" they're going to observe in answering any question they may be asked. For example, they may decide that women must pull on their ears before answering, begin each answer with "the," or cover their mouths with their hands after each answer.

Have the "outsiders" come in and begin asking women questions about themselves. The outsiders can confer about what they notice in the answers. Play until the outsiders figure out the law and then let them each choose a person as a replacement.

• • •

Name That Person

Would you expect to find "Clay" making pottery? Or how about "Rose" working in a florist shop? This is a fun activity all about the meaning of names.

Pass out the "Names!" handout that follows, and then have girlfriends compete to see who can come up with the most names. After about 10 minutes, call time and see how everyone did.

Supplies

• *photocopies of "Names!" handout*
• *pens and pencils*

Answers:

Name That Girl...*1) Melody; 2) Dawn; 3) Pearl; 4) April, May, or June; 5) Candy; 6) Sandy; 7) Pat, Margie, or Marjorene; 8) Lisa or Aleesa; 9) Rose, Violet, Lily, or Daisy; 10) Constance; 11) Fanny; 12) Joy, Gladys, Mary, or Merry; 13) Charity or Sharon*

Name That Guy...*1) Stu; 2) Jack; 3) Woody, Buzz, or Chip; 4) Nicholas; 5) Clay; 6) Bill; 7) Scott; 8) Chuck; 9) Marlin; 10) Barry; 11) Frank; 12) Cliff; 13) Curt an' Rod*

Names!

Instructions: Some names just seem to fit who people are or what they do. How many names can you think of that match these descriptions? Write them on the lines following the clues.

Name That Girl...

1. who sings well_____

2. who gets up early_____

3. who lives in an oyster_____

4. who lives on a calendar_____

5. who's sweet_____

6. who lives on the beach_____

7. who lives in a butter dish_____

8. who rents out apartments_____

9. who lives in a flower garden_____

10. who's always consistent
_____

11. who cools everyone off_____

12. who's a very happy person_____

13. who gives away her possessions_____

Name That Guy...

1. who's in a pot with carrots and potatoes_____

2. who lifts a car_____

3. who lives in a sawmill_____

4. who gave all his change away_____

5. who makes pottery_____

6. who's always in the mailbox_____

7. who lives in a paper-towel dispenser_____

8. who's tossed into a meat grinder_____

9. who swims the ocean_____

10. who grows on the bushes_____

11. who always says what he thinks_____

12. who lives on the edge_____

13. (twins) who are always near a window_____

Word Relay

NO PREP

This is a game you can use anytime and anywhere, and it is great for when you are short on prep time.

Have girlfriends form a circle. Explain that the object of the game is to create the longest sentence possible and to avoid being the person who names the last word in a sentence. Each person can only contribute one word at a time.

For example, the first person can start with any word she wants, anything from "the" to "every" to "flower." The next person must then add a word that continues the sentence without completing it. So, if the first word were "flowers," the next person might add the word "are," and the next person could say, "growing." This sentence could be over at that point, unless the circle continues the sentence. ("Flowers are growing in the field next to my neighbor's house…" or whatever your group comes up with!) Each person who ends a sentence gets one point. The object is to finish the game with as few points as possible.

Top Ten Lists

This is a simple icebreaker that is easy to prepare and also shows just how creative girlfriends can be!

Supplies

• *various objects as described in the game*

Hold up an object, such as a peanut, a coin, or a stone, and ask your girlfriends to think of 10 things they could do with the object.

For instance, a peanut can be a marker on a board game, shot out of a straw, crushed to make peanut butter, rolled with your nose in a relay game, and so on. Encourage creativity!

Continue holding up objects, and see what creative ideas everyone can come up with.

Instant Replays

Icebreakers

Supplies

- *chairs*
- *digital camera*

To begin this game, form two teams. One will be the Sculpture Team, and the other is the Viewing Team. Place four chairs in a line at one end of the room, and have the Sculpture Team create the first "girlfriend sculpture." The Viewing Team will need to look away from the Sculpture Team as they create their work of art.

Allow one minute for the Sculpture Team to arrange themselves in any way they choose on the chairs (including where each person sits or stands, where they place their arms and legs, and what expressions they wear).

Once arranged, have the Viewing Team turn and look at the sculpture for 15 seconds. During this time, take a picture with your digital camera of the girlfriend sculpture. At the end of 15 seconds, call time and have the Viewing Team turn around so they can't see the sculpture any longer.

When the Viewing Team is turned around, have the Sculpture Team rearrange themselves in a *new* way (changing seats, position of legs and arms, expressions, and so on). After one minute, have the Viewing Team turn around once more and then work together to arrange the sculpture back into its original form.

When they think they have it (or after about three minutes), call time and compare the current sculpture with the photograph to see how closely they came to getting the sculpture back into its former position.

Then switch roles so both teams have a chance to show their creativity and form a girlfriend sculpture.

Rubber Band Faces

Don't be afraid to try this fun icebreaker with your girlfriends, as the laughter is well worth it!

Supplies

• *large rubber bands*

Hand each girlfriend a large rubber band. Then instruct everyone to put the rubber band around her head—between the nose and upper lip, over the ears, and around the head. Got it?

Then when you say "Go," have them try to get their rubber bands from where they are (below their noses) to below their chins without using their hands or any other object—using tongues and teeth is allowed. The first person to get her rubber band below chin level wins. As you can imagine, this creates a lot of funny faces and laughter.

Matching Pairs

Supplies

- *sheets of paper*
- *marker*

This game is similar to Concentration and can easily be altered to fit your group or event. It will not only help girlfriends learn each other's names, but it will remind them of some incredible people from the Bible.

Before the game, write on sheets of paper, in large letters, the names of several Bible pairs, with one name per sheet. You might use some pairs from the following list:

- Adam and Eve
- Cain and Abel
- Noah and the Ark
- Abraham and Sarah
- Isaac and Rebekah
- Jacob and Esau
- Paul and Silas
- Samson and Delilah
- David and Goliath
- Mary and Joseph
- Mary and Martha

Choose two volunteers to be your guessers. Everyone else should line up facing the guessers. Give one name sheet to each girlfriend, making sure each name has a match, but mix them up amongst the girlfriends. Have the women holding the papers keep the papers facing their bodies so the guessers cannot see them.

Have the guessers take turns calling out the names of two girlfriends to try and match the Bible pairs. When a woman's name is called, she must reveal the name she is holding. If the Bible names don't make a pair, the woman turns that paper back to face her so the guesser can no longer see it. Once a pair has been matched, the girlfriends bearing the names of the matched pair should sit down.

After all pairs have been matched, select new volunteers, and have girlfriends play the game again.

For a variation, you can use names from entertainment (such as Penn and Teller, Lois and Clark, Katharine Hepburn and Spencer Tracy) or any other famous pairs (Lewis and Clark, Robert E. Lee and Stonewall Jackson, Orville and Wilbur Wright).

Match It Up! Mix It Up!

Supplies

- *index cards*
- *pens or pencils*
- *two bags*

Game Tip:

If you want to play additional rounds, have girlfriends come up with their own phrase starters.

Give each girlfriend four index cards and a pen or pencil. Have them fold each card in half, as if it's a little book. On the first inside page of each "book," have girlfriends write one of the following phrases:

- If you have a cold, you should…
- When I eat chocolate chip cookies, I like to…
- The best way to catch a frog is to…
- The key to growing beautiful flowers is to…

Then on the second inside page, opposite the first, have girlfriends complete each phrase. It's important that girlfriends don't share their answers!

When everyone has finished, have girlfriends tear their cards in half to separate the "phrase starters" from the "phrase enders." Place all phrase starters in one bag and the phrase enders in the other. Have girlfriends take turns drawing one from each bag and reading the mixed up beginnings and endings. You'll hear statements such as, "When I eat chocolate chip cookies, I like to…go to a muddy place and say 'ribbit.' "

Sound Bite

NO PREP

It's time to use your imagination!

In this game, every girlfriend thinks of a famous person and a three-word quote that will help identify the person. The quote can be either a real statement from history or an imaginary quote that acts as a clue to the person's identity.

For example, maybe the person is a historical personality (Abraham Lincoln: "Fourscore and seven…"), a movie character (Arnold Schwarzenegger: "I'll be back!"), or a Bible character (Noah: "On the boat!").

Have girlfriends take turns giving clues as the other women try to guess the character's identity.

As a fun variation, have women identify the famous person by using three words that suggest the person's identity, rather than using quotes.

For example, Abraham Lincoln might be described with these three words: "Gettysburg," "tall," and "president."

What if You Were a Shoe?

NO PREP

If your group has been together for a while and knows each other well, this is the perfect game for you to play.

Have girlfriends form a circle, and have one person be "It." Ask that person to leave the room. While she is out of the room, have the remaining girlfriends choose a mystery woman.

When "It" returns, have her ask questions about the mystery woman, such as "What if this woman were a color? What color would she be?" or "What if this woman were a shoe? What kind of shoe would she be?" After each question, girlfriends must choose an answer with characteristics similar to the mystery woman. For example, if the woman is cheerful, she might be the color yellow. Or if she is athletic, she might be a Nike tennis shoe.

Have group members answer the questions, and then have "It" guess the mystery woman. Whether the guess is right or wrong, have the mystery person reveal herself. This woman is "It" for the next round of play.

Some other possible objects for the question "What if this person were a...?" could include the following: animal, automobile, body of water, boat, chair, household appliance, flower, piece of clothing, kind of music, type of house, vegetable, tool, kind of transportation, or kind of art.

Icebreakers

Picture Pass

Supplies

- *paper*
- *pens or pencils*

This is a bit like the old game of Telephone, but with a twist. Have girlfriends sit in a large circle (facing outward), and give each person paper and a pen or pencil. Whisper to one person in the circle an item for her to draw (no letters or symbols allowed). You'll want to begin by choosing simple objects to draw, such as a tree, a ball, a hat, shoes, or a book, and then move on to more difficult items, such as a hurricane, a rock, a puddle, a shelf, or a snowball.

On "Go," that woman quickly draws the item and then passes the illustration to the person on her left. Then that person looks at the illustration and draws a new version of what she believes the picture illustrates. If a woman doesn't know what the picture is, she must do the best she can to copy the illustration. Then the second person passes *only her illustration* to the next person to copy (no tracing allowed). Continue until the last person in the circle is passed a drawing. That person must then try to guess what the item is.

Win, Lose, or Mold

Supplies

- *molding clay*
- *3x5 cards*

Ever heard of the game "Win, Lose or Draw"? Here's a funny variation your group will love to play. Instead of *drawing* topics or items, you *mold* them out of clay.

On separate 3x5 cards, write one of these Bible topics: "Noah's ark," "David and Goliath," "serpent," "manger," "empty tomb" and "Jonah and the whale" (or add others you think of).

Form two teams of equal number, and give each team a lump of clay. Place the cards facedown between the two teams. A person on one team chooses a card and molds the clay into a shape to help her teammates guess the topic. No verbal communication is allowed between the molder and the guessers, and writing letters or numbers in the clay is not allowed. Teams take turns molding and guessing the topics. Keep track of the correct guesses. The team that guesses the most topics wins.

Award cans of modeling dough to the winning team members!

Tell Me More!

NO PREP

Just to be different, find the person whose birthday is closest to Christmas and have her start this game. Ask her to think of an adjective, such as textures, sizes, colors, smells, and so on. She should share this word with everyone.

The next person must think of an object with that property and then add another word that would describe the object. Here's the key: Players may not tell what item they're thinking of!

As girlfriends add descriptive words, the objects they're individually picturing will change. For example, if the first woman says "pink," and others have then added the words "living" and "small," the next player might be thinking of a pig and add "noisy." The first person may have had a flower in mind, so when play comes back around, she will have to think of a new object that fits all the descriptions.

When a player can't think of an item that might be described that way, she says, "Tell me more!" and the last person to add a word must tell what object she was thinking of. If neither of these players can add a word that describes a real thing, have the last player tell what item she was thinking of when she added her last word, and then start again with a new word.

A Penny for Your Thoughts

Icebreakers

Supplies

- *newsprint or poster board*

Game Tips:

If a girlfriend doesn't have any money with her, have her borrow a coin from a friend.

Since all the money will be mixed up at the end, you can suggest collecting it all and donating it to a charity. No one will be out more than a dollar, so most people will agree. If anyone really wants her money back, be sure to give it to her.

Before your meeting, write the following statements on a sheet of newsprint or poster board:

$1: Name one prayer God has answered for you.

25¢: Tell what you want to be doing 25 years from now.

10¢: Name 10 things that give you joy.

5¢: Name five things you do well.

1¢: Tell one nice thing someone has said to you this week.

When girlfriends arrive, have them each select one coin or bill not greater than one dollar from their wallet or purse.

Call out an amount of money, such as $1.35, and have girlfriends form groups whose money total is equal to or within 25¢ of that amount. See which group came the closest to the amount you called (everyone can cheer for that group!). Then have each woman in the group use the chart you've created on newsprint or poster board as a prompt for what she should share with the rest of the group.

After everyone has shared, have girlfriends trade money with someone else, and call out a new amount ($2.41, $1.83, or whatever you want!). Each time new groups are formed, have girlfriends answer the question that corresponds to their money, and then trade before the new round begins.

Greatest Game Ever

Supplies

- *a variety of objects as described below*

If you're like most of us, you have a room full of miscellaneous stuff that's been collected over the years, and you're not quite sure what to do with it. Well, here's a solution.

Before your meeting, gather a variety of objects, such as:

- a banana
- empty 2-liter bottles
- a stuffed animal
- one sock
- a box of macaroni
- hymnals or song books

Put all of this stuff on a table in front of the room. When everyone arrives, have women form groups of no more than four, and then have a representative from each group choose one or two items for her group. (If you have enough objects, have participants choose another item until all the objects are taken.)

The object of this activity is to work together to create an entirely new game that uses the objects teams have selected. Give teams 10 minutes to invent the game and practice playing it so that they know how it works.

When everyone is ready, have each foursome take turns teaching its game to another group. Repeat for as long as time allows. You may come up with the world's greatest new game!

Count Your Blessings

Supplies

- *paper*
- *pens or pencils*

NO PREP

Remember the old song, "Count your blessings, name them one by one…?" Well, here's a fun way to do just that.

Form teams and give each team a sheet of paper and a pen or pencil. Have women tally points according to their answers to these statements:

- Add your team members' ages.

- Give 20 points for each person whose birthday is in December or January.

- Give 5 points for each person who made her bed this morning.

- Give 1 point for each brother or sister each person has.

- Give 1 point for each book of the Bible your team can name.

- Give 10 points for each person whose first name can be found in the Bible.

After teams tally their points, have them divide the total by the number of people in their team. Then see if each woman on the team can think of that same number of gifts God has given her. It's a fun challenge!

● ● ●

The Marvelous Hat

Supplies

- *a crazy hat*

How many times have you wished, "If only I could…" Well, here's your chance to share those ideas with your girl-friends and see what fun ideas you come up with.

For this activity, you'll need to bring a crazy hat from home. Give it to a girlfriend and ask her to put it on, and then ask her to talk about something in our world she would change if she had the ability to do it. That person then throws the hat to someone else, who then shares about what she would change. Continue until everyone has had a turn.

What Do You Know?

Supplies

- *poster board*
- *markers*

This Jeopardy-style game, involving little-known facts about your girlfriends, is a real unity builder! You can play it over and over, using information about different group members, and the novelty will never wear off. Your group will love it.

The week before you play, interview several girlfriends, asking them fact-based questions that most of the other women in your group wouldn't know. For example: "Where were you born?" "Where would you most like to visit?" "What awards did you win in elementary school?" and "What is your dog's name?"

Place the questions on poster board or newsprint in columns under the women's names with headings such as "Family Life" and "Free Time." Each row of questions under the columns should have different point values—give lower point values to the easier questions and higher point values to the tougher questions.

Have girlfriends form two teams and take turns answering the questions to see how much they know about their fellow group members. Interviewed women can play, but they can't answer questions about themselves.

The Hot Seat

Supplies

- *chairs*

This activity is for groups who really want to have depth in their relationships, and the topics discussed can go anywhere.

Sit in a circle around an empty chair. Ask for a volunteer to sit in the hot seat. Ask this girlfriend to tell about a time in the past week she experienced God's presence. Then ask others to sit in the hot seat and share. You can use a variety of questions for this activity, including these: When was a time last week when you roared with laughter? What was the topic of the last serious discussion you had with someone close to you? In what way did you come to the aid of someone last week?

You don't have to think of the questions yourself—let the group members suggest questions for the hot seat.

Roving Bingo

Supplies

- *photocopies of the "Roving Bingo" handout cut into sections*
- *pens or pencils*

In this variation of Bingo, girlfriends get to know each other a bit better.

Before the meeting, photocopy and cut apart the sections of the "Roving Bingo" handout. You'll need one section for each girlfriend. You can give each person a copy of the same section, distribute several different sections among participants, or play four different rounds, using a different section for each round.

To begin, give everyone a pen or pencil and a section from the "Roving Bingo" handout. Tell girlfriends they are to find others who can sign their names to and answer the questions for each square. Each person may not have the same person sign her card twice, and girlfriends will only have four minutes to finish, so they need to work quickly.

After four minutes, call time. Ask girlfriends how many squares they got signed, and then ask them to share some of the things they discovered about each other.

Roving Bingo

Around the House

_____owns an umbrella. What color is it? Where did you get it?	_____drinks at least two glasses of water a day. How many glasses do you drink total? What's your favorite soft drink?
_____likes to stay up late. What's your favorite late-night activity? What's your favorite late-night snack?	_____skips breakfast every morning. When do you eat a morning snack? What do you eat?

Beach Bums

_____has found a sand dollar on the beach. Where was it found? When was it found?	_____has swum in the Pacific Ocean. When were you there? Why were you there?
_____ wears a swimming cap. What color is it? Why do you wear it?	_____has been skinny-dipping. Where were you? Who was with you?

Vacation Relaxation

_____has visited a factory while on vacation. Where were you? What did you sample?	_____vacationed at home. Did you clean while home? What else did you do?
_____has traveled overseas. How long were you there? Who was with you?	_____has taken a cruise. Where did you go? Did you eat a midnight meal?

Buffet Line

_____ could eat pizza every day. What's your favorite topping? From where?	_____likes vanilla ice cream. What's your favorite topping? Cone or cup?
_____prefers pie over cake. Fruit or cream? A la mode or plain?	_____ doesn't eat meat. For how many years? Do you eat fish?

The Early Years

Do you have a baby picture of yourself that family have "oohed" and "aahed" over for years? Well, here's an opportunity to show off what a cute baby you really were!

A week prior to your meeting, ask the women in your group to each bring a baby picture of herself, taken before she turned 2. Before the meeting begins, write "The Early Years" across the top of the poster board, and attach the baby pictures of your group members, identifying each one with only a number.

Distribute paper and a pen or pencil to each girlfriend, and have each person list down the left side of the paper the numbers you used on "The Early Years" board. Have girlfriends now look closely at the board and guess who is in each picture. Allow them about two minutes to write names next to the numbers. When two minutes are up, identify the group member in each baby picture, allowing girlfriends to "grade" their papers to see how well they did. You can offer a prize to the person who got the most right and to the woman whose picture stumped the most people.

Supplies

- *baby pictures of participants*
- *poster board*
- *marker*
- *tape*
- *paper*
- *pens or pencils*

Balloon Bouquets

We all love to get a bouquet of flowers every now and then. The thoughtfulness of the giver makes us feel special and valued. Here's a simple way to remind your girlfriends how God gives us special moments each week, showing his love for each of us.

Have the group sit in a circle, and ask girlfriends to gently bat around a large 11-inch (or larger) balloon. When you yell, "Grab it!" the person nearest the balloon should grab it. Ask that woman to tell about a time in the past week when she felt lifted up by a person or experience. Then bat the balloon again, and go through the process with a new person.

Supplies

- *11-inch or larger balloon*

Chapter 3
Games With a Purpose

Do you need a game to help illustrate the point of a lesson? Or maybe an activity that will be affirming and build unity among the girlfriends in your group? This chapter is full of ideas for activities that "make a point" on all kinds of topics regarding human relationships and our relationships with God.

Picture Pieces

Supplies

• *paper and pens*

In life, things don't always turn out like we expect. Use this activity to start a discussion on trusting God in all things.

Have women sit in a circle, and give each person a piece of paper and a pen. Ask them to write their names on their paper and then begin to draw something. Have each woman think about what the final picture will look like. Then have them pass the papers to their right and add some artistic details to the new papers. Remind them that they are trying to make a picture. Keep passing until the pictures return to their original artists.

Go around the circle, and have each woman show her picture and say what she first had in mind.

Spirit Balloons

Use this simple balloon activity to help women tell each other about the twists and turns of life.

Supplies

- *balloons*
- *black markers*

Give each participant a balloon and a black marker. Have them inflate their balloons, hold them closed at the necks without tying them, and write their name on their balloon.

Have everyone release the balloons at once, asking everyone to keep an eye on her balloon as it flies throughout the room. When all the balloons have landed, have each woman retrieve her balloon and stand wherever it landed. Ask the women to form groups of four or five with people who are standing closest to them. Have them talk about dreams they once had that didn't pan out or about how some aspect of life hasn't turned out the way they expected.

Design~Your~Own Obstacle Course

This game calls for plenty of room, creative ideas, and lots of energy!

Supplies

- *newsprint*
- *pens or pencils*
- *various obstacles such as chairs, tables, boxes, ropes, athletic equipment, and blankets*

Game Tip:

If you have a small group or a small room, you may want to have girlfriends design an obstacle course as one large group rather than break into small groups.

You will want to have participants form groups of three to five. Explain that each group will create an obstacle course for the other groups to follow. Show them the obstacle supplies available for groups to use to create their courses. As groups will set up their courses one at a time, they can plan to use all the supplies available if needed.

Give each group a piece of newsprint and a pen or pencil. Have each group design its own obstacle course and draw a diagram of the course on the newsprint. Groups should include at least four stations in their courses and use only the supplies provided.

When all groups are finished designing their courses, have them take turns setting up their courses and leading the other groups in completing them.

This is an activity that can be used to illustrate and begin a discussion about the obstacles that women face in life, such as fear, temptation, worry, and anger.

Big Challenge Mini~Golf

See how this mini-golf game can launch a discussion about God's plans for us.

Supplies

- *two bags*
- *40 paper cups*
- *40 paper plates*
- *four pairs of scissors*
- *masking tape*
- *newspaper*
- *20 straws*
- *toy golf sets*
- *markers*

Put together two bags, each with the following items: 20 paper cups, 20 paper plates, two pairs of scissors, masking tape, newspaper, and 10 straws.

You'll also need toy golf sets with balls and clubs, which you can purchase from a dollar store or borrow from a local mini-golf course.

Have your girlfriends form two teams, and give each team a bag. Tell each team that their job is to create a five-hole miniature golf course using the items in the bag to create obstacles. They must use cups for each hole, number the holes for order of play, and determine the par for each hole.

When teams have finished building their courses, have each team begin play on the opposing team's course. Award prizes for best team score, best individual score, worst individual score, most creative putt, play of the day, or most creatively designed hole.

After the game, discuss the similarities between our plans for our lives and God's plans for us. Ask women how God's plan is like following a course they didn't design, how they overcome course obstacles, how perseverance makes a difference, and how teamwork helps.

Games With a Purpose

Compass Journey

Supplies

- paper
- pen or pencil
- compass for each group
- end of trail marker
- photocoies of typed instructions

This is an activity you can use to begin a discussion about our journey through life and what we can use to help us find direction as we travel a sometimes rocky and winding road.

In preparation for this activity, you will need to plot out a compass course outside, preferably in a large area. To do this, mark a beginning point, holding a compass in your hand, and step off any number of paces, keeping track of your direction. As you create your journey, record the number of paces you make on a piece of paper, as well as any changes of direction you may make along the way. Place a marker at the end of your course.

After plotting your course, type up the instructions and make a copy for each group.

To begin the game, have your girlfriends form groups of five to eight. Give each group a compass and a copy of your instructions. Send out the groups in five-minute intervals, seeing if the groups can make the same journey you did and locate your marker.

Once everyone has taken the journey, gather back together as a large group, and talk about the journey. What are the things we use as compasses today? What guides our lives? Who helps us on our journeys?

One Body, Many Parts

Supplies

- markers
- newsprint
- tape

Working together, making decisions, and appreciating others in the body of Christ can sometimes be a challenge. Use this activity to discuss the importance of unity.

Have each girlfriend choose a partner, and provide each pair with a sheet of newsprint and a marker. Allow each pair a minute or two to decide on a scene from a Bible account. Once all partners have decided on their scenes, tell partners they may no longer speak to each other. Have each pair work together by holding the same marker to draw their scene. Limit the drawing time to five minutes.

Once everyone is finished, tape or tack the pictures to the wall, and have everyone see if they can figure out what scene each pair was drawing.

Gift Givers

This is a fun way to spark friendships and inspire getting-to-know-you conversations.

Take your group of girlfriends to a mall (now you know this is going to be fun!), and begin a discussion on gifts and their significance. You might want to set a coffee shop or the food court as your meeting location.

Then give each woman the name of someone else in the group—preferably someone she doesn't know well. Send women out into the mall in pairs to find gifts for their assigned people, using the following rules:

- You can't spend more than five dollars for a gift.
- You can only tell your partner whom you're shopping for.
- You have to return with your gift in 30 minutes.

When all the girlfriends have returned, have them take turns presenting their gifts to the recipients, explaining why they purchased the gifts. Ask women to each say the following as they give their gifts: "[Name of recipient], this gift is to remind you of how valuable you are to God and to this group."

This activity works well to encourage new friendships and to provide tokens of remembrance.

Silent Cake~Bake

Supplies

- *fully equipped kitchen*
- *recipes and ingredients for cakes or cake mixes*

Game Tip:

Using a cake mix is acceptable, but making one from scratch will make more of an emphasis on the theme.

This activity can be used to begin a discussion on several different topics, such as communication with others and God, how we face challenges in life, or teamwork and working together.

You will need to either meet in a home or use the kitchen in your church. Supply the ingredients women will need to make cakes. Have women form groups of three, and then tell them that their goal is to create a cake without speaking. Explain that teams must decide what kinds of supplies to use and how they'll work together to make and bake the cake as a team. The only catch is that no one may utter even one word during the whole experience.

Once the cakes are in the oven and are baking, talk about the experience, its challenges, and what the women learned through participating. When the cakes have cooled, add some frosting and enjoy a yummy treat!

Name Tag Mixer

Supplies

- *blank name tags*
- *pens*
- *photocopy of the rules*
- *bowl or container*

You can use this game to begin a discussion on how each person's gifts are needed in the body of Christ.

Prepare by photocopying the handout and cutting where indicated. Fold these slips and then put them into a bowl or other container.

Give each woman a blank name tag and a pen, and explain that the goal of this mixer is to have their names written on their name tags by the end of the game—but they need to follow all the rules to make this happen.

Have each girlfriend pick one of the slips of paper. This paper describes that person's "unique ability" to complete a task. Women will mingle to find others with unique abilities that will help them complete their names, and at the same time, they'll help others complete their names.

Use this game to remind women that just as each person's unique ability is necessary to complete a name, so in the body of Christ, each person is uniquely gifted by God and needed for the wellness of the whole.

Name Tag Mixer

You can only draw vertical lines. (For example, the letters "b," "d," "h," and "k" all have vertical *parts* that you can draw, but you can't draw the entire letter.)

You can only draw horizontal lines, but you can't cross "t's." (For example, the letters "e," "f," and "z" all have horizontal *parts* that you can draw.)

You can only dot "i's."

You can only cross "t's."

You can only draw curves, not circles or lines. (For example, the letters "c," "e," "j," and "r" all have curved *parts* that you can draw.)

You can only draw angled lines. (For example, the letters "k," "v," "w," and "y" all have angled *parts* that you can draw.)

You can only draw circles. You may not draw partial circles, only complete circles. (For example, the letters "a," "g," "o," and "p" all have circular parts that you can draw.)

You can only draw capital letters. You can draw only one capital letter for each person.

Games With
a Purpose

Faith Will Find It

Supplies

• hidden objects as described in the game
• checklist of items hidden

Use this twist on I Spy to lead women into a Bible study about seeking and finding God.

For this activity, you'll want to choose a living room or meeting room that has lots of knickknacks, pictures, or decorations. Choose a dozen or more items that can be easily hidden in the room (place a toothpick in the groove of a wooden frame, place a clear marble in the bottom of a glass goblet, attach a matching color of yarn to a lampshade, and so on).

Have girlfriends form pairs, and give each pair a checklist of the items. Let them know that everything's in plain sight but not easily spotted at a glance. Set a time limit, and tell pairs to check off each item as they locate it. When time's up, discuss questions such as these:

- If God wants to be discovered and known, why is the search often difficult?

- In comparison to the effort you exert in other areas of your life, how much energy do you put into seeking God?

- What's one way that you've discovered God in your life recently?

Thankful Penny Toss

Supplies

• pennies
• a cup or saucer
• masking tape

This is a game of skill, but it's a skill you'll be hard-pressed to use!

Place a cup or saucer on the floor, and lay a length of tape about 6 feet from the cup.

Give each girlfriend an equal number of pennies. Allow them to stand at the line of tape and practice tossing pennies into the cup. Once they have gotten the hang of hitting the mark, ask them to take turns tossing their pennies into the cup, and have them say something they are thankful to God for as they toss each penny.

You can also use this game as a way to start a discussion on missing the mark in life or aiming for goals that are difficult.

Sightless Sandwich Maker

Supplies

- *ingredients and utensils to make several sandwiches*
- *table*
- *blindfolds*

This is a game that makes quite a mess, but it is a fun way to introduce the ideas of trust, worrying about things we cannot see or control, and communication.

Before the game, you will need to set out sandwich-making ingredients and utensils on a table. (Remember to be aware of allergies women in your group may have, such as nut or wheat allergies!)

Have girlfriends form teams of three. Assign one person in each team to be blindfolded, one to sit quietly somewhere along the edge of the room, and the other to act as a guide.

To begin, each blindfolded girlfriend should go to work making a sandwich, with the guides talking their partners through the process. While they can talk to their partner, they cannot touch or help her in any way. When a sandwich is done, the guide should give the blindfolded person verbal directions to help her locate their third teammate. When they've reached the third girlfriend, the blindfolded partner should feed her the sandwich. No one may touch the sandwich but the blindfolded woman, and she must be guided only by words.

You can change roles at this point until each person has done one role (and has had her sandwich!). Then open your time up to discussion based on where you want your session to go.

Games With a Purpose

All for One

NO PREP

If you are entering a discussion on resolving conflict, this is a simple activity you can use.

Invite women to form groups of four. In this game, all four women must agree on one thing. For example, you might ask what snack food they enjoy. Each group must find an answer each girlfriend agrees on. If even one person doesn't agree, they must find another answer. This isn't as easy as it sounds!

Read each of the following phrases aloud, and allow time for each group to agree upon an answer:

- something you like to do when you have free time
- a snack food you like to eat
- a story of Jesus you like
- a place you like to go for fun
- a holiday you enjoy
- a TV program you enjoy

What's It Worth?

Supplies

- *index cards*
- *several markers*
- *a table*
- *various items such as a bag of M&M's*
- *a can of fruit*
- *a bag of balloons*

If you're a fan of *The Price Is Right*, you'll enjoy this game that easily leads into the topic of worth and the importance of accurately understanding how God values his children.

Write the price of each object on an index card, and line up the items on a table. Place each index card facedown on the table under the appropriate item.

Have women form small teams. Give each team a stack of index cards and a marker. Explain that you're going to play a game similar to *The Price Is Right*. As a team, they have to guess the price of each object and write it down.

The team with the best guess—without going over—wins that item and they can share it or enjoy it as they like.

Jelly Bean Times

Supplies

- *jelly beans*
- *bowl*

Game Tip:

You can also use M&M's or Skittles for this, but as some of the colors are different, you will need to make adjustments on the color/ emotions used.

Who knew that jelly beans could spark such interesting conversation?

Before your meeting, place jelly beans in a bowl. As you get started, pass the bowl to each woman, and have her take out a few, but instruct that these jelly beans are not to be eaten…yet.

Each woman will have jelly beans of various colors. Explain that each color represents a different emotion:

Yellow = fear,

Red = embarrassment,

Green = envy,

Blue = sadness,

Purple = anger,

Black = loneliness,

Orange = happiness,

Pink = love, and

White = courage.

Give everyone a few minutes to choose one of her jelly beans, and then go around and have everyone share an experience related to that emotion.

This is an activity that not only encourages listening but encourages sharing from the heart, and it strengthens the emotional ties among the participants.

Games With a Purpose

Balloon Blitz

Games With a Purpose

Supplies

- *balloons*
- *trash bags*

It's common for women to feel too busy. This is a great activity to start a discussion on priorities and how easily life can become too busy.

Before the game, inflate and tie off one balloon for each woman. Put all the inflated balloons in a trash bag. If you have a large class, you may need to use several bags. Have women join you in forming a tight circle.

Take out one balloon, and tap it to the woman beside you. Explain that the goal of the game is to keep the balloons moving and up in the air at all times. If a balloon hits the ground, the nearest person should pick it up and keep it moving.

Have women continue tapping the balloon to each other while you add more balloons. See how many balloons the women can keep going before the game reaches total chaos. Once the game is out of control, collect the balloons and begin again.

Encourage women to name the balloons for the many activities they have to juggle in real life!

"Dear Abby"

Supplies

- *several advice columns*
- *3x5 cards*
- *pens or pencils*

Use this game to introduce the topic of wisdom or using discernment when seeking advice.

Before your meeting, search your local newspapers and clip three or four appropriate advice columns (such as "Dear Abby") that deal with issues relative to women.

In your meeting, pass out pens or pencils and blank 3x5 cards. Read one of the problems, but don't read the advice that was given. Give women a few minutes to think about the problem and write their advice on their cards. Encourage them to include any Scripture references that relate to the situation.

When everyone is done, collect the cards and read a few of the responses out loud, allowing time after each response for women to discuss the advice. Finally, read the advice given in the newspaper, and have participants talk about whether it was good or bad advice.

Gifted

Supplies

- *marshmallows*
- *toothpicks*

Game Tip:

You can also use gumdrops and toothpicks to construct your models.

This game can be used to illustrate how each Christian has a unique gift and is necessary to the body of Christ, as well as to reinforce the importance of communication.

Have girlfriends form groups of five. Give each group a supply of marshmallows and toothpicks. In another room or somewhere out of sight, have a model constructed out of marshmallows and toothpicks.

Each group member has only one role to play. Here's the breakdown:

Player 1—Can only use her right hand and can only handle toothpicks.

Player 2—Can only use her left hand and can only handle toothpicks.

Player 3—Can only use her right hand and can only handle marshmallows.

Player 4—Can only use her left hand and can only handle marshmallows.

Player 5—This girlfriend is the Runner and is the only person allowed to see the model in the other room, as well as the only person who's allowed to speak. She instructs the other group members in constructing a replica of the model but isn't allowed to touch anything.

Be sure to enforce all the rules, especially the talking one, and see how well the teams can replicate the model.

Games With a Purpose

Oddball Bowling

Use this game to introduce topics related to things that throw us off course, such as sin or temptation, or to discuss the importance of patience and determination.

Supplies

- *volleyball*
- *small bag of sunflower seeds or candies*
- *nine empty two-liter plastic bottles*
- *duct tape or packing tape*

Before the game, use duct tape or packing tape to secure a small bag of sunflower seeds or small candies to the side of the volleyball to make it unbalanced so it will roll erratically. You can also use a small bag of unpopped popcorn or nuts, as long as it adds enough weight to one side of the ball. When everyone is ready to play, have girlfriends form two teams, and have them line up at opposite ends of the playing area.

Set up the nine two-liter bottles like bowling pins in the middle of your playing area, only set them up in a square. Give the volleyball to the first girlfriend in line at one end of the room, and have her roll the ball and knock down as many pins as possible.

Have the first person in line at the other end of the gym retrieve the ball and roll it back at the pins. Keep alternating teams until all the pins are down. Then reset them and have girlfriends go at it again until everyone has had a turn.

Faith Adventures

Our faith truly is an adventure. Here's a powerful activity to remind your girlfriends of God's unfailing love during every part of their journey.

Supplies

- *items girlfriends bring with them*

Have girlfriends each bring an item that represents a powerful event in their faith journey. It could be a picture from a retreat, a baptism certificate or a devotion booklet. If they don't have an item, girlfriends might "bring" a memory, such as when a friend invited them to church for the first time.

Have girlfriends form a circle. One at a time, have them each show their item and describe the powerful event in their faith journey. This is a great way to introduce a time of thanking God for that powerful event in their faith adventure.

Your Chair, Please

Game Tip:

For every six women you have, set up another row of chairs. As you're rolling the die and calling out the numbers, all the teams will have to work fast to keep up with you.

This game is designed to get women thinking about and discussing the idea of humility, what it means to put others first, and situations where women have to make that decision.

Before the game, place six chairs in a straight line facing the same direction. Have six women sit in the chairs, and then number off from one to six. The goal of the game is to be in the number six chair (the highest number).

Explain that in this game they will be putting others before themselves. Tell them that you'll roll the die and say what number comes up. The woman sitting in the chair with that number may ask the player in the chair with the next highest number to switch places. That player can decide if she wants to switch places or not. Since there's no number seven chair, the woman in the number six chair can ask to switch places with the person in the number one chair. Let them know you will roll the die 10 times and then stop to see who is in the number one chair at the end of the game.

Roll the die and call out the number rolled. Pause after each roll as women ask each other to switch places. The faster you roll numbers, the faster the action as women scramble to get the seat with the lowest number.

End with discussion on how women decided whether or not to switch places, how they decided whom to ask to switch places, and so on.

Games With a Purpose

Do You Know?

NO PREP

This is an effective activity for illustrating how little we can really know about our friends, even if we spend a lot of time together. It can also be used to begin a discussion on how deeply God knows us, even when others don't.

Have women form pairs with someone they don't know very well. Explain that you are going to give them three minutes to learn as much as they can about their partner.

After three minutes, have everyone form a circle. Go around the circle, asking one partner in each pair the first question from the list below. If the partner doesn't know the answer to the question, she can make one up. After each partner answers, have the rest of the women vote on whether the answer was correct or not. Then have the second partner tell what the correct answer is. After one person from each pair has answered the first question, ask the next question about the opposite partner in each pair. This isn't a game for keeping score—just have fun with it.

Questions to use:

- What color is your partner's favorite food?
- Who is your partner's biggest hero?
- How many lipsticks or lip balms does your partner have in her purse right now?
- What was your partner's first car?
- What is your partner's favorite comic strip?
- Can your partner do a handstand?
- What brand of toothpaste does your partner use?
- What did your partner want to be when she was younger?

After partners have answered a question, have them turn and tell what they learned that was the most interesting.

Take Your Pick

NO PREP

This is a fun way for girlfriends to get to know more about the interests of each other, and it is a game that can be used to delve into deeper topics, such as morality, faith, and ethics.

This can easily be played in pairs, trios, or larger groups, depending on your number of participants. In the game, group members take turns asking each other questions that require the person answering to make a choice. For example, girlfriends might have to decide between…

- ice cream or pizza,
- the beach or Disneyland,
- reading a book or putting together a puzzle,
- swimming laps or lying in the sun,
- cats or dogs, and
- getting up early or late.

You can easily turn this game into a discussion of faith and moral issues by asking other types of questions. For example, girlfriends might have to decide between gossiping and sharing the problems of another, or keeping someone's confidence.

Be sure girlfriends have the opportunity to explain why they chose one thing over another. After you've provided a few questions, take turns letting group members think up items, destinations, or activities for others to choose between.

Games With a Purpose

Praying for Others

Games With a Purpose

Supplies

- *a smooth stone for each person*
- *permanent markers*
- *paper bag*

Use this activity to encourage girlfriends to pray for each other throughout the week.

Give each woman a stone and a marker. Have them each write on their stone the name of a friend or family member for whom they've been praying.

Put the stones in a paper bag, and have each person reach in and pick a stone. Explain that they are to carry this stone to remind them to pray for the person named on it. Starting the following day, if they happen to meet a person from your group, they are to trade stones and pray for the person on the new stone. Ask girlfriends to keep praying for the person named as long as they have the stone, and remind them to bring the stones to your next meeting.

At the next meeting, have girlfriends each tell about their experiences of praying for these people. Also have them tell any answers to prayer for the people whose names were written on the stones.

Positively Promising

Supplies

- *copies of the handout cut into strips*
- *scissors*

This game requires lots of mingling and helps remind women how God promises to meet their every need. It's a truly affirming activity that encourages women to look into God's Word for answers.

Beforehand, photocopy the handout provided and cut it into strips so each strip includes either a "positive" or "negative." You should have enough so every woman gets two strips. Make sure each strip has a match, and keep a master list for yourself.

Hand one positive slip and one negative slip (but not a matching pair) to each woman. Then tell each person to find the positive statement for her negative by asking others what they have. When women find their matching pair, they get to keep them (their original positives go to the people who have the matching negatives).

After everyone finds a match, gather in a circle and take turns reading each negative, followed immediately by its positive.

Positively Promising

Negative: I'm so tired.

Positive: I will give you rest (Matthew 11:28-30).

Negative: Nobody really loves me.

Positive: I love you (John 3:16).

Negative: I'm not smart enough.

Positive: I give you wisdom (1 Corinthians 1:30).

Negative: I can't do it.

Positive: You can do all things (Philippians 4:13).

Negative: I'm afraid.

Positive: I have not given you a spirit of fear (2 Timothy 1:7).

Negative: I feel all alone.

Positive: I will never leave you or forsake you (Hebrews 13:5).

Negative: I'm always worried.

Positive: Cast all your cares on me (1 Peter 5:7).

Clay Creations

In this game, girlfriends will create miniature sculptures to represent their relationships with God.

Supplies

• *modeling clay or dough*

Ask girlfriends to form groups of three, and give each group one ball of clay or half a can of modeling dough. Explain that girlfriends are to take turns in their groups creating sculptures that portray their relationship with God. They then can show these sculptures to each other.

Girlfriends will each have 60 seconds to create a sculpture. Then the other two group members will have 60 seconds to guess what the sculpture represents. If no one guesses correctly in 60 seconds, the sculptor should tell or reveal what it is.

Encourage girlfriends to answer the following questions once their sculpture has been identified:

• In what way does your sculpture represent your relationship with God?

• If you could change any part of your relationship with God, what would it be?

Games With a Purpose

Tell Me More

Quite often we forget to tell our friends the things that we appreciate about them and what makes them special to us. This activity can be used to build unity within your group and to remind each other of the positive qualities girlfriends appreciate about each other.

Supplies

• *crayons*
• *paper*

To begin, give each girlfriend a different colored crayon and a sheet of paper. Tell them they're going to take some time to "doodle" things that represent each other's good qualities, such as a face with two open eyes to represent someone who always gives her full attention.

Encourage girlfriends to mingle, and ask them to each doodle positive qualities on at least five other people's papers. As a girlfriend draws a doodle, have her explain the doodle by verbally completing this sentence: "I like the way you _____ because _____." Tell girlfriends that they can't draw the same doodle more than once—they must all be different.

Chapter 4
Just for Fun

Get ready for fun! The activities included in the following pages are action-packed relays, scavenger hunts, contests, and simply crazy games. You can use these at retreats, showers, or a girlfriends' night out. Beware, these games will have everyone laughing and acting silly like you've never seen before!

Postcard Paste~Up

Supplies

- about 40 picture postcards
- scissors
- tape or stapler
- basket
- pens or pencils
- card table
- postage stamps

Before this game, you'll need to collect about 40 picture postcards and cut each one in half. Place a card table with one-half of each postcard, a stapler or some tape, and a few pencils in the center of the room. Place an empty basket beside the table.

Hide the other halves to your postcards all over the room and anywhere else you want the participants to go.

On "Go," have girlfriends race to find the hidden postcard halves. When a girlfriend finds a hidden half, she must run back to the table, staple or tape it to the other half, sign it, and "mail" it in the basket.

When all the cards are mailed, count who found the most. Give that woman a prize of postage stamps!

My Problem

To begin this game, form two teams of equal size. Each team sits in rows facing each other. Give each person a paper and pencil. Ask those on one side to write down some great predicament they might imagine themselves in. For example, you leave the house and realize you have on one black shoe and one blue shoe, or you have a flat tire on the way to a job interview.

Those on the other side, without communicating with the first team, should write down a solution to some predicament, such as take two aspirin and call me in the morning, or add more flour.

After everyone has written down a predicament or a solution, the first girlfriend in line one states her predicament. Then the girlfriend opposite her says the solution she had written down. This continues until everyone has had a turn. The results are hilarious!

Hold~Your~Breath Relay

This fast-paced relay is breathtaking!

Have your group form relay teams. Designate a color for each team. Then give each participant a straw and a piece of paper that matches her team's color. On "Go," team members will each run in turn from one end of the room to the other, using their straws to suck and hold their papers. Teams score one point for every paper they can carry across the room and drop into a basket. If a team member drops her paper, she is out. After everyone has run the relay, the team with the most points wins the game.

Game Tip:

Try this variation: Everyone moves her paper across the room at the same time. If women drop their papers, they pick them up by sucking on their straws and then continuing on. The team that finishes first wins the game.

Just for Fun

Find That Picture

This is a game of high energy and competition!

Have the participants form four groups, and have one group go to each corner of the room. Give each group a stack of magazines and newspapers, and then stand in the middle of the room.

Say, "You're in a race against the other groups to find a picture of what I call out and bring it to me. You can't just rip out the whole page—you have to rip out just what I called out. Even if another group *finds* it first, the winner is the first person to get the picture to me."

Once groups are ready, yell out a picture for them to find and bring to you. When one group has brought you that picture, call out another item. Continue until participants are tired of playing or their magazines and newspapers are all torn up.

Here are some ideas for pictures or text you might want to have teams look for:

- the letter "m"
- a politician
- an athlete
- the score of a game
- a shoe
- a movie star
- a graph or chart
- the name of our town
- a famous person under the age of 20
- a greasy food
- a cold beverage
- cereal

Just for Fun

Feed Your Face

Supplies

- *paper bags*
- *a variety of food items as described in the game*

Game Tip:

While it can be amusing, don't put anything in the bag you wouldn't be willing to eat yourself (so no onions or strained prunes!). Also, be aware of allergies women in your group may have, such as nut or wheat allergies!

Form teams with an equal number of girlfriends on each team. If that isn't possible, one of the team members must go twice. Each team will have a paper bag that contains items such as a peanut butter and jelly sandwich, a banana, a jar of baby food, a lollipop, etc. The bag must contain one item for each person on the team, and all bags should have the same items in them. Team members must not see what is in the bags.

The bags are placed across the room from each team. On a signal, one member of each team runs up and grabs something from the bag. She must not be able to see what there is to pick. She must eat every single bite of the item before she runs back and tags the next member. The team that is finished first with everything wins.

Refrig~e~raider Party

NO PREP

This idea may be a stretching exercise for some girlfriends, but it's a great way to "come as you are." The next time you and your girlfriends are looking for something new for a get-together, try a "refrig-e-raider" party. It requires no advanced planning (something we all love) and lots of surprises!

Ask each girlfriend to raid her refrigerator before coming and to bring something found there. No fair spending the afternoon in the kitchen whipping up something special! The idea is that you bring whatever you already have on hand and share the fun as well as the food.

Possibly you'll end up with an assortment that ranges from leftover meatloaf to cheese to cake. More than likely, you'll be surprised to find that you have all the ingredients you need for a meaningful get-together.

Board Game Tournament

This tournament works best if you use games that everyone is familiar with, such as Yahtzee, Monopoly, Jenga, Boggle, Pictionary, and so on.

Before girlfriends arrive, you'll want to set up tables in a circle or square with chairs on all four sides of each table. Mark each chair at each table with a different color of tape or paper. So you might have a green, black, red, and yellow chair at each table. Put one game on each table (along with paper and pencils if those are needed for that game).

After all girlfriends have arrived, have everyone take a seat.

Explain to the women that players will play the board game in front of them until you call time after 10 minutes. At that time, you'll call out directions for moving to a new spot based on the color indicated on the chairs. So after the first 10 minutes you might call out, "Everyone sitting in a chair with a green marking move one table to the left. Everyone sitting in a chair with a red marking move one table to the right." Those players will move and join in the game with the two remaining original players, picking up where the last players left off and continuing the game.

After 10 minutes, call out different movements, such as black moving one table to the left and yellow moving one table to the right. Don't have more than two players per table move at one time. Mix up the movements so everyone gets to know new people, play different games, and have a lot of fun!

Bringing Up Baby

Whether you are at a baby shower or a retreat, this game will have everyone in stitches.

To begin, have women form four teams, and give each group a baby doll, a baby bathtub or basin full of water, shampoo, a towel, a cloth diaper, ointment, baby powder, two diaper pins, and a doll outfit. Explain that in this game, each person is allowed to use only one hand—the hand she doesn't normally write with. Teammates must decide how to work together to care for their "baby."

Teams must accomplish these tasks in order: Bathe the baby and shampoo its hair (without letting it drown), dry the baby (remembering, of course, to support its head), rub ointment on the baby's bottom and powder it, pin a diaper on the baby, and dress the baby.

The team of girlfriends that completes this challenge fastest is the winning team.

Musical Chairs Dress Up

This is a hilarious way to have a fashion show like you'll never have again!

Set up chairs in a large circle, facing the center, making sure there is one fewer chair than girlfriends. In the center of the circle, place a large pile of old clothes (like boots, hats, helmets, suits, sports equipment, dresses, and shorts).

Begin as you would Musical Chairs, with participants walking around the circle until the music stops, and then everyone racing to find a chair. Except in this game, whoever doesn't find a chair must put on a piece of clothing from the pile in the center. Everyone gets to stay in the game! When all the clothes in the center are gone, you can have quite a funny fashion show!

Wacky Relay

This is just a fun relay race that will have everyone cheering and laughing by the time it's done.

Supplies

- *3x5 cards*
- *two chairs*

Set up two chairs at one end of the room. On each chair, place a stack of 3x5 cards on which you've written relay instructions participants will carry out (see the samples below) and which you have shuffled (so instructions are in a different order for each team). You'll need one set of instructions for each team participating.

Have women form two teams, and have them line up in single-file lines on the side of the room opposite the chairs. On "Go," the first person on each team will run to the chair, take one card, follow the instructions, tag the chair, run back to her team, and lock arms with the next person in line. Both of them will then run back to the chair, choose another card, follow the instructions together, tag the chair, lock arms again, run back to their team, and lock arms with the third person, and so on. This continues until all team members have been included, finished the instructions, and run back to their starting line.

You can use the following relay instructions, or come up with some on your own:

- Sing "Jingle Bells."
- Do five jumping jacks.
- Run around the room, touching each corner of the room.
- Take off your shoes.
- Run backward to your team.
- Get a drink of water from the nearest sink or drinking fountain.
- Hop to your team.
- Run around the chair two times yelling the name of your church.

Indoor Blind Croquet

Supplies

- *several croquet sets*
- *squares of craft foam*
- *miscellaneous items as described in the game*
- *blindfolds*

This is a game that's fun at a winter retreat or any meeting where you just want to laugh. You'll need several croquet sets if you have a large group.

To set up the course, anchor the wickets in squares of craft foam, and set up the game in a traditional pattern in your fellowship hall, gym, or other large room. Or you could use the whole building to create a course that's more like miniature golf, incorporating "creative" obstacles! You might push chairs together to form arches, use extra-large mailing tubes for tunnels, or stack books in the middle of the course as hazards.

Once the course is set up, the game is quite simple. Have girlfriends form pairs, and give each pair a blindfold. One partner must wear the blindfold, and only this person may hit the ball. The other partner gives instructions but can't touch the mallet or the ball. Have players switch the blindfold every other turn so they both get turns as the player and as the guide.

The winning team is the pair that completes the course in the fewest number of strokes.

Potato Promenade

Supplies

- *a small potato*
- *stopwatch or watch with a second hand*

Game Tip:

If you have a large group, form several groups, giving each group its own potato.

This game provides a personal challenge as well as the opportunity to cheer for others.

Have girlfriends from two groups, and have these groups stand in lines at opposite ends of a large room. Take a potato and demonstrate the following procedure.

Place your feet closely together. Set the potato on top of your feet. Carefully shuffle your feet so you move forward, keeping the potato balanced on the tops of your feet.

After everyone has seen your demonstration, give the potato to the first person in one of the lines. The idea is for this person to shuffle along to the first person in the opposite line, pass off the potato, and then have that person shuffle back to the next person in the first line. Keep track of the time it takes for everyone to promenade with the potato, then have girlfriends play again, racing against their previous time.

Happy Hooping

Supplies

- *Hula-Hoop*

This game poses a problem that can be made easier as team members work together.

Have girlfriends form a line, holding hands with those on either side. Give the first girlfriend a Hula-Hoop, and explain that she must pass her entire body through the hoop then pass the hoop down the line so it goes over the body of the next person, and so on. What makes this difficult is that the chain of hands must never be broken! It's a challenge for participants to get their bodies through the hoop when they can't let go of those beside them.

Play several times, timing how long it takes for women to get the hoop from one end of the line to the other. As they continue to play, women may realize the hoop will move faster if they help each other, and that they don't have to stay in a straight line. This means those on the ends with free hands can help those in the middle.

If you have a large group, you can split into teams and have them race against each other, seeing who can get the hoop from one end to the other the fastest.

Musical Grab Bag

Supplies

- *grocery bag*
- *miscellaneous items as described in the game*
- *radio or CD player*

This is a game that will leave everyone talking and laughing long after it's over.

Fill a grocery bag with varied weird stuff, such as pantyhose, lipstick, old neckties, slippers, crazy glasses, strange hats, earrings, shower caps, and buttons.

Have girlfriends sit in a circle. Begin playing music, and have participants pass the bag until you stop the music. Whoever's left "holding the bag" reaches in without looking and has to put on whatever she pulls out. Keep playing until all the items are being worn.

Be sure to get a group picture afterward.

Toilet~Paper Relay Run

Supplies

- *roll of toilet paper for each team*

You've probably used toilet paper to create a wedding gown at a bridal shower and maybe even used a few rolls to decorate someone's house when you were young and wild, but most likely you have never used it in a relay race.

For this relay, you will need to form two teams and have these teams form two lines, side by side, at one end of the room. Designate a line at the other end of the room as the finish line. Tell girlfriends they will need to stand with their legs apart, facing the finish line. Give the first person in each line a roll of toilet paper.

The goal of the game is for girlfriends to wrap the toilet paper around their teammates' ankles and then race to the finish line without breaking the strand. They can wrap the toilet paper however they wish, as long as each ankle has been wrapped with toilet paper at least once. Additionally, they must, at all times, maintain at least an arm's length away from the person in front and behind them. If the strand breaks at any time during the race, the team must return to the beginning, rewrap the toilet paper, and start again.

The first team to successfully cross the finish line wins!

Pantyhose Blast

Supplies

- *pantyhose*
- *potatoes*
- *empty cans*

Ah, pantyhose, the bane of every woman's existence. In this game, pantyhose are finally used for something fun and creative.

To begin, give each woman one pair of pantyhose and a small potato. Have participants tie one leg of their pantyhose around their waist with the extra leg hanging down their back. Then insert a potato into the dangling leg.

Have women line up facing a row of empty cans. One at a time, have them knock over as many cans as possible by swinging their potato back and forth through their legs. The only rule is they may not use their hands at all.

If you have a large group, have two women play at a time.

The winner is determined by who can knock over the most cans. Give the winner all the leftover potatoes.

Have a camera on hand for this one—it's hilarious!

Quick Change

If you and your girlfriends are ready to have a zany night full of laughter and lighthearted competition, this is the game you're looking for!

For this game you will need several items of oversized clothing, such as overalls, a shirt, socks, big boots, and a large hat.

Prior to the game, gift-wrap a prize in a small box. Place this box inside a larger box, and gift-wrap it again. Continue this until you have gift-wrapped it four times.

Have girlfriends form a circle, and place the clothing and gift box in the middle of the circle. Hand the pair of dice to one of the participants, and explain that she will roll the dice and then pass them to the next woman, who will roll the dice and pass it to the next person, and so on.

If a woman rolls doubles, she should pass the dice and run to the middle of the circle where she will begin putting on all the clothes. When she is wearing all the clothes, she can begin unwrapping the present. Meanwhile, the other women will continue rolling and passing the dice. If someone else rolls doubles, she will come to the middle of the circle. The first woman will remove the clothes as quickly as possible so the second woman can begin putting them on, and then the first woman will return to her seat.

The game continues until someone finally unwraps the present and is declared the winner.

Supplies

- *oversized clothes*
- *gift wrap*
- *tape*
- *boxes*
- *prize or treats*
- *one pair of dice*

Just for Fun

Beach Ball Basketball

Supplies

- *two sets each of scuba goggles and flippers*
- *two beach balls*
- *broom*

Game Tip:

If you don't have access to a basketball court, you can set up a target women have to hit with the beach ball, or put a laundry basket at the end and have them toss the ball from a line into that basket.

This low-cost, low-prep game will give your non-basketball players a chance to score points, although they may look a little silly doing it.

Have women form two teams of equal number. Give each team one pair of scuba goggles, one pair of flippers, and a beach ball. You can find these items in the toy department of many stores.

The object of the game is for team members to run with the ball, one at a time, from one end of a basketball court to the other while wearing the scuba gear. Have them stop at the free-throw line and attempt to score a basket with the beach ball. Have a volunteer stand by the nets with a broom to poke the ball out of the net if a basket is made. Then the player races back to her team, and the next player dons the scuba gear, runs to the free-throw line, and so on. The team with the most points after everyone has a turn, wins.

Skit Tag

NO PREP

Even the most familiar Bible stories become novel in this just-for-fun game that's similar to Telephone.

Form five or six small groups. Call the first group into a different room while the rest of the groups do something else. Instruct the first group to make up a short two- to three-minute silent skit based on a given Bible passage. When they're ready, have this group perform the skit in front of everyone, but the second small group needs to pay close attention—as they'll need to get up and repeat that skit immediately! Have the second group perform the skit, as they remember it, in front of everyone, with the third group doing the skit as they remember it right after that. Continue until all the groups have done their version of the skit. By the time the last group performs, the skit is usually hilariously different. Have the last group perform the skit for the entire group, and then have the first group perform the original skit again.

Just for Fun

Snap! Crackle! P...uzzle!

Supplies

- *several cereal boxes*
- *scissors*
- *cereal*
- *bowls*
- *spoons*
- *milk*

No one can forget the jingle to their favorite childhood cereal, and many of us remember it well from watching Saturday morning cartoons! Here's a creative way to use those memories and the cereal we all loved.

Cut off the front panel of several cereal boxes—one for each group you want to form. Then cut up each panel into puzzle shapes—one for each person you want in that group. Mix together all the pieces from all the cereal boxes, then give one piece to each person. On "Go," have girlfriends race to find the people with the pieces necessary to complete their puzzle.

When all the cereal box panels have been assembled, have groups discuss the following questions:

- What was your favorite cereal as a child?
- What's your favorite cereal slogan or jingle?
- What cereal name are you most like and why?
- If you had an ad slogan or a "list of ingredients" for yourself, what would it be and why?

End the discussion time with snacks—cereal, of course, and don't forget the milk!

Ping~Pong Pass

Supplies

- *Ping-Pong balls*
- *8-ounce clear plastic cups*

If your space is limited but you want to have a silly relay race, this is the game for you!

Have girlfriends form two or more equal teams, and have each team form a straight line. Give each person one cup, and give the first team member in each line a Ping-Pong ball.

Tell girlfriends to hold their cups in their mouths (the easiest way is to bite the cup where the side and bottom meet). Then have the first team member place the ball in her cup. On "Go," she must pass the ball down the line from one cup to another until it reaches the last team member.

Some ground rules: Women can use their hands only if they need to adjust their cup—and only if they *don't* have the ball. A team must start over if someone does use her hands while in possession of the ball or if someone drops the ball at any time.

To add challenge, have girlfriends pass the ball down the line and back to the beginning again before you declare a winner.

Plas~Toes!

Supplies

- *a plastic glove for each player*

Have all the players remove their shoes and socks, and give each woman one plastic glove. While seated in a chair or on the floor, have everyone compete to place her glove onto one foot, right or left, as if it were being put onto a hand. It doesn't matter where she begins, but the thumb portion of the glove must always be placed onto the big toe.

Play a couple of rounds, then heat up the competition and find the overall winner. This time women can't use their hands. Instead, they must put the glove on with the other bare foot! Hands may only be used to support their body. This is a real challenge, but it's always hilarious. You might want to take photos so girlfriends can have proof of their new talent.

Line~Up

NO PREP

This is a fun game of giving opinions and feelings that can go as quickly or slowly as you want.

Indicate that one end of your room is 1, the middle is 5, and the other end is 10—on a rating scale with 1 being worst and 10 being best.

Explain that you are going to call out some questions (see below). Everyone will stand where they want depending on how they want to answer the question. If their answer is "awful," they'll stand on the 1. If their answer is "wonderful," they'll stand on the 10. If their answer is "average," they'll stand on the 5. They can also stand in the areas in between, depending on how strongly they feel about their answer.

When you have read a question and everyone is on their number of choice, ask them to turn to the person next to them and quickly explain why they chose to stand where they did.

Here are some questions to get you started:

- How was your last vacation?
- What do you think of golf?
- What do you think of chocolate?
- How much do you like to exercise?
- How do you feel about classical music?
- How was your week?
- How do you feel about reading?
- How do you feel about your family?
- How do you feel about prayer?
- What do you think of God as your Father?

Just for Fun

Bible Treasure Hunt

Supplies

- concordance
- Bibles
- colored envelopes
- paper
- pen or pencil
- a prize for everyone

Looking for a way to get everyone up and moving around? Use a concordance to locate verses in the Bible that describe various locations in and around your church. Look for words such as *entrance, table, fountain* (for drinking fountain), *curtain, altar, trees,* and so on. Write out the Bible references on separate slips of paper. Place each slip of paper in an envelope, and hide all but one of the envelopes at the various locations, making sure you don't put the verse at its actual location.

If you have a large group, have girlfriends form teams, and place two, three, or four colored envelopes at each location (depending on the number of teams). Teams will read the clue in their own colored envelope.

Hand girlfriends a Bible and the envelope you didn't hide. Have them read the reference aloud and begin to search, as teams, for the next envelope clue. The Bible reference in each envelope will lead the players to the next clue. At the last location, have some treats waiting as a treasure!

Your Nose Knows

Supplies

- paper towels
- small candies as described

Give each player two paper towels and 25 to 30 tiny candy pieces (such as Red Hots or M&M's). Ask group members to spread themselves out around the room so everyone has plenty of room. Tell women to place one paper towel flat on the floor and put the candy pieces on top of it in the middle. They can save the other towel for later.

Explain that the goal of this game is to see who can spell a word the fastest using the candy to form the letters. But here's the catch: You can use only your nose to push the candy into position! Hands may be used to hold the paper towel in place—but *not* to move the candy. Have everyone practice this new skill by writing her name.

When everyone's ready, have them gather all their candy pieces into the middle of their paper towels. Begin by saying simple words for women to spell, and then move to more challenging words, like *cat, dog, exit, fluff, laugh*, or *quirk*. When you're finished playing, have women use the extra towels to clean their noses—they're gonna need it!

Chain Relay

Here's a different twist on a relay race that will give new meaning to the idea of teamwork!

Supplies

- *masking tape*
- *paper*
- *newspaper*
- *rubber bands*
- *scissors*
- *marshmallows*
- *balloons*

Game Tip:

If you have women who cannot physically do somersaults, replace this with another task to be done in unison, such as all drink glasses of water at the same time.

There are two differences between this and an ordinary relay. First, instead of team members performing individually, they are all joined at the hands (secured with masking tape), and therefore, they must do everything together. Second, instead of performing tasks in a given order, the different tasks are at stations around the room, and teams may try them in any order they wish (except for the final task).

Teams of three women join hands to form a line. You will need to stick the joined hands together by wrapping them with masking tape. This is to ensure that the group stays together—if the tape is broken, you'll know the hands came apart.

There must be at least two more tasks than teams. Use tasks that require two hands. Some suggested tasks:

- Fold a paper airplane.
- Cut out a circle from a piece of paper.
- Roll up a newspaper, and put a rubber band around it.
- Untie and tie the shoe of the middle person.
- Feed each member of the group a marshmallow.
- Inflate and tie off a balloon.

Final task: The whole team must do a somersault together without breaking its grip.

There are only two rules to this game:

1. The final task must be done last.

2. If a grip is broken, the whole team must return to you to have the grip retaped before continuing.

Just for Fun

Name That Commercial

This is a fun game that will allow girlfriends to show just how culturally aware they really are!

Before your meeting, use a tape recorder to capture portions of at least 20 radio and television jingles. Record short snippets of the commercials, and be sure not to record the name of the product being advertised.

Have girlfriends form teams of no more than four, and have teams sit in circles around the room. Play the commercial snippets one at a time. The first person to stand gets to guess the product (everybody else sits down before she answers). If she's right, that woman's team wins a point. If wrong, the next person to stand may guess. Continue until someone guesses the product or until all teams have tried. Then move on to the next snippet.

The team with the most points at the end of the game wins. Award an appropriate prize to the winner, such as one of the products from your commercial snippets.

Game Tip:

You can also play this by recording commercials from your television onto a video. Show the video, and the first player to correctly call out the name of the product being advertised wins that round.

Hall of Fame

Just for Fun

If your group likes Charades, then they'll really get a kick out of this game.

Pick a volunteer to begin building a "Hall of Fame" by pantomiming a famous person or musician of her choice (no words). All other girlfriends try to guess who the person is. Whoever guesses correctly gets to pantomime next.

After performing a pantomime, a player can't guess for the remainder of the game and is now considered a part of the Hall of Fame, but that doesn't mean the fun is over. Whenever another player begins to pantomime, all previous pantomimers should sing or talk like their famous person, which creates quite a distraction and lots of laughter.

Of course, the excitement builds until there is only one player left. This person must quiet the group by calling out each person individually. Once called, the person nods off to sleep (no snoring!), and the final person can complete her pantomime.

Charade Twists

NO PREP

Everyone loves to play Charades, and they are such a great barrier breaker. We've all played traditional Charades, so try these versions:

• *Go for It*

In this moving version of Charades, a girlfriend can either stay put and act out a word or run to find something in the church (or meeting place) to help act it out. For *soap opera*, for example, she can run to a bathroom, grab some soap, then pretend to sing dramatically.

• *Stumpers*

Each team thinks of words for the opposite team to act out, and the goal is to stump the other team. To make things even more interesting, limit some rounds to just nouns or just verbs. Some favorite stumpers include *oysters* and *appendage*.

• *What Am I?*

Team members must act out nouns by becoming them. Start with easy words, such as *dog* and *cheerleader*, then move to harder words, such as *dinosaur* and *candle*.

• *Sound Effects*

Players can make as much noise as they want to act out words such as *garbage disposal*. For more laughs, combine Sound Effects Charades with another version.

Balloons and Backs

Supplies

- large 11- or 16-inch balloons
- chairs

If there are balloons, you know it's going to be a fun relay! Here's an idea that will have everyone working together and cheering for her team.

Form two teams, and then tell teams to divide into trios. If there are an uneven number of people, then some people will have to go twice to even out the trios. Have teams stand at one end of the room, and place a chair for each team at the opposite end.

Give each team a balloon. Direct the trios to stand back to back, lock arms with the other two members, and then place the balloon between their backs.

Explain that the object of the relay is for teams to get to the chair at the other end of the room and back without the balloon getting away. They then pass the balloon to the next trio and the race continues. If the balloon escapes, that team is out of the race. The first team finished wins.

Zip, Zoom, Zowie

Supplies

- chair

NO PREP

Women may need to let go of some inhibitions for this game, and it's all for the fun of the race!

Form two teams of equal number. Have them form two single-file lines on one side of the room, and place a chair or some other object at the other end.

This is a relay of creativity. Women will each select their own way of getting to the chair and back, but each one must move in a way that hasn't been used before. They can hop on one foot, hop on two feet, run, walk backward, skip, walk heel to toe, somersault, or do any other movement as long as no one else has done it before.

To add a sense of urgency, time the race. Then hold a second relay to see if they can improve on their first time. During the second round, tell women that they can do the relay any way they want, whether someone has done it before or not.

Balloon Limbo

Supplies

- *a long pole or rope*
- *several inflated balloons*

Game Tip:

Keep extra inflated balloons on hand in case balloons pop.

You might want to get some Hawaiian shirts for your girlfriends to wear for this game.

Lay the pole in the center of the room. Have girlfriends form two teams of equal size. Have half of each team line up on one side of the pole and the other half of each team line up on the opposite side—all lines should stand 10 feet from the pole.

With another person, hold the pole horizontally 5 feet from the ground. Give an inflated balloon to the first woman on each team on one side of the pole. Have them each place the balloon under their chin and hold it to their chest.

On "Go," have these people race to the pole and "limbo" under it (bend backward as they walk under the pole), then have them each pass the balloon to the first teammate in line on the opposite side of the pole. Players must pass the balloon from chin to chin—no hands allowed. If a girlfriend drops her balloon, she must return to the front of her line and begin again. Have all team members shout the "limbo-ing" person's name as encouragement. The first team to finish wins.

Run the relay several times, lowering the limbo pole each time to see who's the most limber limbo team.

Just for Fun

Novel Quest

This is by far the funniest and craziest "scavenger hunt" you and your girlfriends will ever play!

You will need to use a large room for this game. Have women form groups of six to 10, and have each team find a separate place to stand or sit in the room. Place a masking tape X in the center of the room (or, if you have more than four teams, make one X for every two teams, keeping the X's several feet apart). Prepare point tokens, such as tickets, slips of paper, beans, or play money.

Tell women they're about to go on a scavenger hunt inside the room. You'll call out things for teams to find or a description of an object, and then teams are to figure out what object in the room matches that description. As soon as a team finds the object, it is to send a representative to stand on the X (if you are playing with multiple X's, continue to play until all the X's are covered). The team that gets to an X first with the item that matches the description will get a token. At the end of the game, the team with the most tokens wins!

Read the following clues one at a time:

- a ring you don't wear on your finger (earring)
- a face without any hands (a watch)
- pictures of three political leaders (could be on coins or currency)
- a script of the movie *The Ten Commandments* (the Bible)
- a source of illumination (a flashlight, a match, or an illuminated watch face)
- the official seal of your state or province (check your driver's license)
- a camera
- a ticket or ticket stub
- a pair of sandals
- two things that are heeled (two feet, socks, or someone's shoes)
- exactly 67 cents
- pianos have lots of these…bring only two (keys)
- one person with three ponytails

Total teams' points, and then award the winning team with a prize they can share.

Supplies

- masking tape
- tickets or point tokens as described in the game
- prizes

Game Tip:

If you are playing with more than four teams, you can give a token to the first two or three teams that make it to the X. This will keep everyone scrambling even after the first team has received their token.

Gimme Five!

NO PREP

This is a game that everyone will love playing and will really get girlfriends laughing and having fun.

Have women form groups of three, and explain that the object of this game is for groups to try and name five items in a category that you will call out. When members of a trio can name five items, they need to jump up and yell, "Gimme Five!" Then trio members will share the items they came up with so the rest of the group can verify them. When a trio has five verified items in the category, they've won that category.

Use the categories listed below, or create your own.

- clothing designers
- rodents
- discount stores
- kinds of rooms in a home
- sports that do not use a ball
- animals smaller than a dog
- old wives' tales
- things in a classroom
- animals bigger than a squirrel
- famous sayings
- fruits
- coffee drinks
- candy bars
- types of makeup
- insects

Group Impressions

If you have a few drama queens, this game will have you laughing for sure.

Supplies

- *a bandanna or flag*
- *sheets of paper*
- *black markers*
- *candy*

Before the game, select four or six judges, and position them on the stage facing the audience. Give each judge a black marker and as many pieces of paper as you'll have rounds of the game.

Introduce the judges as international experts who will determine scores for the performances they're about to see, much as Olympic judges rate a performance as an 8.5 or a 10. The decision of the judges is final.

Divide your audience into two teams. Explain that team members are to work together to pantomime a series of actions. When you announce the impression, teams will have 15 seconds to do it. When you drop the bandanna or flag, teams are to stop the impression.

Judges will assign one score for each impression based on (1) the inventiveness of the impression and (2) the extent of team participation.

Assign an equal number of judges to each team, and then have teams perform their pantomimes. To keep scoring fair, have judges switch teams after each round. Use the following ideas:

- You're sitting in the most boring church service in the history of the world.
- You're in a movie theater watching the saddest movie you have ever seen.
- You ate in the hospital cafeteria, and you're dying of food poisoning.
- You're attending an art gallery, but you don't understand any of the paintings.
- You're presenting the keynote speech at the International Mime Convention.
- You're a jockey in the Kentucky Derby, and your mount is about to win the race.
- It's open microphone night at the Elvis Impersonator Cafe, and you're onstage.
- You're a six-pack of soda that has been shaken so hard that your tops are popping.

Total the scores and give the winning team chocolate to share.

Chapter 5
Seasonal Games

Christmas is almost here, and you need an activity that will get everyone in the spirit of the season. Or Valentine's Day is approaching, and you want to take part in the fun but don't want to just focus on those who are married or have a "significant other." Or you're having a New Year's Eve party and need a fun game to play. Go ahead and browse through this chapter to find something you can use to celebrate just about any season.

Easter Egg Hunt

Supplies
- plastic Easter eggs
- candy
- flathead nails
- strip of leather
- coins
- a communion cup
- a communion wafer
- thorns from a rose

Give the traditional Easter egg hunt a twist by using egg-fillers that are meaningful and make a powerful reminder of Christ's sacrifice.

Prior to your meeting, place candy inside some of the eggs, and in others, place flathead nails, a strip of leather, coins, a communion cup, a communion wafer, and thorns from roses (available from a florist). Also leave some of the eggs empty (signifying the empty tomb). Then set up a maze-type area outside, and hide the plastic eggs.

Then, of course, have women go on an egg hunt. Once the hunt is over, gather women together and have them open their eggs and discuss each item and the role it played in Christ's death and resurrection.

Pop, Pull, and Surprise

Add a bang to your New Year's activities!

For this game you'll need to purchase party-favor crackers from a party supply store. Inside each "popper," insert a clever question, a funny quote, a Charades idea, or a Bible study question. Give one party cracker to each woman as she arrives, or if you're planning a New Year's Eve dinner, place one cracker at each place setting.

Have group members take turns pulling open their party crackers and proceed with any instruction or discussion that the cracker inserts suggest. So if someone pops open a Charades suggestion, be sure that person acts out that Charade. If someone receives a Bible study question or quote, allow time for discussion.

Add this activity to a New Year's Eve party or a small-group session, or simply close your regular meeting with this fun surprise.

Supplies

- party-favor "poppers"
- fun ideas to insert in the poppers

Game Tip:

As an option, you can put additional party favors in the crackers that might relate to your current Bible study or unify your group, such as small hearts to represent your group's love for Jesus.

Jigsaw Jack~o'~Lanterns

This is a great competitive game for the fall season.

Divide girlfriends into teams of two or three, and give each team a pumpkin and a sharp knife. When everyone is ready, give each team only a couple of minutes to cut their pumpkin up into more than 10 pieces.

Teams will then rotate to a different pumpkin. Give each team two minutes to put its "jigsaw puzzle" pumpkin back together again, using toothpicks to hold the pieces in place.

The first team done, or the team with the most "together" pumpkin after the time limit, is the winner. Pumpkins must be able to stand up alone to be considered a winner. This can be a messy activity, but it sure is fun!

Supplies

- pumpkins
- knives
- newspaper
- toothpicks

Seasonal Games

Letters to God

This is a great New Year's activity that requires a little extra work and memory on your part, but the girlfriends in your group will appreciate the encouragement.

Have girlfriends write letters to themselves detailing ways they'd like to get to know the Lord better or ways they would like to grow in the coming year. Here are a few suggestions:

- Begin a regular prayer time each day.
- Commit to read through the Bible in a year.
- Make a list of five people to pray for consistently throughout the year.
- Find a place to volunteer or tutor.
- Send cards of encouragement to friends or family members.

The possibilities are endless! Encourage women to be creative and customize the lists to their talents and gifts.

Encourage girlfriends not to let others see their letters, as these are personal between them and God. After the women are finished writing, have them seal the letters in self-addressed envelopes. Place the letters in a safe place until December 31, and then mail each girlfriend her letter.

Surprises in Disguises

What girlfriend doesn't wish she could look like someone else occasionally? Here's an opportunity to be in disguise and maybe get a laugh or two along the way, which is especially fun around the Halloween season.

Begin by forming two teams. Give each team a set of disguise items, and then send them into separate rooms. Tell them their goal is to disguise one of their members so that the other team can't tell who she is. Have teams each choose a person to disguise, and use the supplies to mask her true identity.

When teams are ready, have them each send their disguised person into the other team's room. That team may look closely at the disguised girlfriend, but no touching is allowed. If the team guesses the person's identity, that team gets a point. If they guess incorrectly, the other team gets a point. Continue playing multiple rounds, and then award a prize to the team with the most points.

Heart~Stopping Stories

This is a silly activity that is easy to prepare and hilarious to listen to.

To prepare for this storytelling game, either invent a story beforehand or read a familiar fairy tale. If you're feeling especially creative, you might even ad-lib this activity!

Ask girlfriends to sit in a circle, and give each woman 10 candy hearts with sayings on them. Then recite your story, stopping at times so women have a chance to complete your sentences with candy-heart sayings. For example, you might say, "When the witch saw Snow White, she said…" A girlfriend might complete the sentence by saying, "Call me" or "Will you be mine?"

Supplies

- *a bag of candy conversation hearts*

Game Tip:

If you have a large group, you might photocopy your story and then have girlfriends break into groups. Have one person in the group read the story and the other women respond with sayings from their hearts.

Red~Hot Fun

This is a fun relay that can easily be adapted to any holiday by simply substituting seasonal candy (candy corn, candy hearts, malt eggs).

Ask participants to form pairs, and hand each pair a paper cup. Have pairs place their paper cups on the floor at one end of the room and then stand at the opposite end. Give each pair 15 small cinnamon candies and four toothpicks.

Have pairs set their candies on the floor in front of them, and then explain that once you say "Go," pairs will have two minutes to transfer all their candies into their paper cup at the opposite end of the room. They might roll their candies or carry them on their toothpicks, but no hands are allowed! They will have to work together on this!

At the end of two minutes, have women count the candies in their cups, and give a seasonal prize to the pair with the most candies in their cup.

Supplies

- *small cinnamon candies (or other seasonal candy)*
- *toothpicks*
- *paper cups*
- *prizes*

Even or Odd?

This is a fun, easy mixer to use around Valentine's Day.

Supplies

- *heart-shaped candies*
- *small sealable plastic bags*

Before your meeting, place anywhere from one to 10 pastel, heart-shaped candies in small, sealable plastic bags—one bag for each person. Vary the number of candies in each bag. As women arrive, give them each a bag, and tell them to count the candy hearts in it.

The object of the game is to get the most bags of candy hearts during a specified time period. Women will get bags by going around the room asking others "even?" or "odd?" They then will either collect or relinquish bags according to the person's answer. For example, if someone asks "even?" and the person she asks has an even-numbered total of candies in her bag(s), the asker gets the bag(s) from that person. But if the person has an odd number of candies, the "asker" must give up her bag(s) to the "askee."

Each time a woman takes someone else's bag(s) of candy, she must add those to her total candies (so her odd or even stance could change).

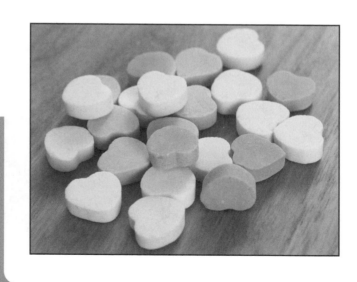

Friendship Garden

This flowery game is perfect for any spring gathering such as Easter, Mother's Day, May Day, or just a celebration of warmer weather and flowering plants.

Have women sit around tables in groups of five or six. Give each group a Friendship Garden Game and paper and pencil. The first woman spins both spinners and follows the directions on both to answer her question. Then she passes the game to the next person, who spins both spinners and follows the directions.

If anyone lands on the same question twice, she can spin again. The goal is to get to know others better and enjoy laughing together. Play as long as time permits.

Christmas~Carol Confusion

Try this hilarious twist of musical fun at Christmas gatherings!

Supplies

- *songbooks*
- *paper*
- *pen or pencil*
- *bowl*
- *Christmas ornaments*

Before your meeting, you'll need to gather songbooks that include religious and secular carols, and select the titles of several carols. Write them on slips of paper, and put them in a bowl.

When girlfriends arrive, have them form trios, and have each trio draw two carols from the bowl. Give them time to practice singing the words of one song to the tune of the other. It takes practice and a little discipline, but the results are worth it when a trio sings "The First Noel" to the tune of "Jingle Bells"!

Award Christmas ornaments to the best performers.

Team Tree Decorators

Do your girlfriends need a little extra something to get in the mood for Christmas? Then this is the game they need to play!

Supplies

- *flashlight*
- *roll of toilet paper*
- *box of tinsel*
- *a few plastic flowers*
- *a bag for each team*

Form teams of equal number. Give each team a bag of the decorations listed. Allow groups to use their scarves, hats, coats, and gloves as additional accessories.

The unique part of this contest is the "tree." Rather than a typical Christmas tree, each team *is* the tree. Give each group five minutes to plan, and then give the command for members of each team to make themselves into a human pyramid, decorating themselves as they go. After a set time, judge the trees and award prizes.

Game Tip:

Since teams may only be able to stay balanced as a "tree" for a few seconds, you might want to take quick digital pictures of each team, quickly pop them up into a media show such as PowerPoint, and show them to the entire group. Great for laughs, and it makes judging easier!

Seasonal Games

Thank~You, Thank~You, Thank~You

NO PREP

Perfect for Thanksgiving season, these thank-yous, given and received, will warm up any cold winter day and draw your girlfriends together in a special way.

If you have a large group, you'll want to have girlfriends sit in circles of 10 to 20. If you have a small group, form one circle. Explain that there are three parts to this activity, and you will give details about each one as you come to it.

Round 1—Have girlfriends each tell about one *thing* for which they're thankful.

Round 2—Have them each name one *person* in the group they're thankful for and why.

Round 3—Have the group say three things they're thankful for about each group member. Here's how to do it: Begin the round by choosing one person to receive the thank-yous. Have girlfriends raise their hands if they'd like to say why they're thankful for that person. Once hands are up, the person you chose should call on three people to speak. The person who's receiving the comments should simply say "thank you" after each person speaks.

Game Tip:

Often there are more than three hands raised, but limit comments to three for each person, as this allows everyone to have a chance at receiving encouragement.

Musical Christmas

Use Christmas songs to launch a musically good time.

Supplies

- *chairs*
- *Santa hat*

Have girlfriends sit in a circle of chairs facing inward, with one fewer chair than there are women. Have the extra person stand in the middle wearing a Santa hat. This girlfriend then stands in front of a seated person, looks at her directly, and sings a line from a Christmas song. The seated woman then must respond by singing the next line of the Christmas song within three seconds. If she is unable to respond correctly, she trades places (and hat) with the person in the middle. The more creative and quicker the person in the middle is, the harder it is for those seated to respond correctly.

Jingle Jumble

Supplies

- *jingle bells*

This idea helps prepare girlfriends for Christmas or possibly caroling around the neighborhood. It's also a fun way to see how many Christmas songs your group knows. You'll need several sets of jingle bells, the kind school bands use. Or use sets of car keys or other noisemakers.

Have girlfriends form teams, and give each team a set of bells. Then rehearse the chorus of "Jingle Bells." Have teams shake their bells as they sing the familiar tune.

After practicing "Jingle Bells" while shaking the bells, explain that you will point to a team, which must sing one verse of any Christmas carol it can think of (except, of course, "Jingle Bells"). When that team is done, you'll motion to everyone to sing the "Jingle Bells" chorus and to shake the bells again. Then point to another team. It must sing a verse of a different carol. If a team can't think of a different carol when you point to it, it's out. The winning team is the last team that can still think of a Christmas carol.

Keep things rolling by allowing only 10 seconds for a team to think of a carol. Happy singing!

Girlfriend Tip:

For more seasonal gathering ideas, check out *Chick Adventures: Wow Events for Women's Groups*. This book has five events themed to different times of the year—and is loaded with fun!

Seasonal Games

INDEX

Index

GAMES BY TOPIC

Index